OXFORD ST

Series Edito

Edward Thomas

Selected Poems

Edited by Steven Croft

Oxford University Press

OXFORD

UNIVERSITY PRESS

Great Clarendon Street, Oxford OX2 6DP

Oxford University Press is a department of the University of Oxford.
It furthers the University's objective of excellence in research, scholarship,
and education by publishing worldwide in

Oxford   New York

Auckland   Cape Town   Dar es Salaam   Hong Kong   Karachi
Kuala Lumpur   Madrid   Melbourne   Mexico City   Nairobi
New Delhi   Shanghai   Taipei   Toronto

With offices in

Argentina   Austria   Brazil   Chile   Czech Republic   France   Greece
Guatemala   Hungary   Italy   Japan   South Korea   Poland   Portugal
Singapore   Switzerland   Thailand   Turkey   Ukraine   Vietnam

Oxford is a registered trade mark of Oxford University Press
in the UK and in certain other countries

British Library Cataloguing in Publication Data

Data available

ISBN: 978-0-19-912980-5

1 3 5 7 9 10 8 6 4 2

Typeset in India by TNQ Books and Journals Pvt. Ltd.

Printed in China by Printplus

Paper used in the production of this book is a natural, recyclable product made from wood
grown in sustainable forests. The manufacturing process conforms to the environmental
regulations of the country of origin.

The publishers would like to thank the following for permission to reproduce photographs:

Pages 2, 16: Mary Evans / Robert Hunt Collection; page 9: E.O. Hoppé / Corbis;
page 12: Getty Images; page 114: Ocean / Corbis; pages 117, 151, 160: Cardiff University
Library: Special Collections and Archives; page 126: Mary Evans / Grenville Collins
Postcard Collection; page 138: Mary Evans / Peter Higginbotham Collection

Contents

Acknowledgements

The text of the poems is taken from *Edward Thomas: Collected Poems*, edited by R. George Thomas (Faber & Faber, 2004).

Extracts from the *Authorized Version of the Bible* (*The King James Bible*), the rights in which are vested in the Crown, reproduced by permission of the Crown's Patentee, Cambridge University Press.

Eleanor Farjeon: extracts from *Edward Thomas: The Last Four Years* (OUP, 1958), reprinted by permission of David Higham Associates for The Estate of Eleanor Farjeon.

Matthew Hollis: extracts from *Now All Roads Lead to France: The Last Years of Edward Thomas* (Faber, 2011), reprinted by permission of the publishers.

Andrew Motion: extracts from *The Poetry of Edward Thomas* (The Hogarth Press, 1991), reprinted by permission of The Random House Group Ltd.

Stan Smith: extracts from *Edward Thomas* (Faber, 1986), reprinted by permission of the publishers.

Helen Thomas: extracts from *As It Was and World Without End* (Faber, 1972), reprinted by permission of the publishers.

Although we have made every effort to trace and contact copyright holders before publication, this has not been possible in all cases. If notified, the publisher will rectify any errors or omissions at the earliest opportunity.

Acknowledgements from Steven Croft

I would like to thank Sandra Haigh for all her invaluable comments and help and support in the preparation of this text. I am also grateful to Jan Doorly for her very helpful advice and sensitive editing of the manuscript.

Editor

Steven Croft holds degrees from Leeds and Sheffield universities. He has taught at secondary and tertiary level and headed the Department of English and Humanities in a tertiary college. He has 25 years' examining experience at A level and is currently a Principal Examiner for English. He has written several books on teaching English at A level, and his publications for Oxford University Press include *Exploring Literature*, *Success in AQA Language and Literature* and *Exploring Language and Literature*.

Foreword

Oxford Student Texts, under the founding editorship of Victor Lee, have established a reputation for presenting literary texts to students in both a scholarly and an accessible way. The new editions aim to build on this successful approach. They have been written to help students, particularly those studying English literature for AS or A level, to develop an increased understanding of their texts. Each volume in the series, which covers a selection of key poetry and drama texts, consists of four main sections which link together to provide an integrated approach to the study of the text.

The first part provides important background information about the writer, his or her times and the factors that played an important part in shaping the work. This discussion sets the work in context and explores some key contextual factors.

This section is followed by the poetry or play itself. The text is presented without accompanying notes so that students can engage with it on their own terms without the influence of secondary ideas. To encourage this approach, the Notes are placed in the third section, immediately following the text. The Notes provide explanations of particular words, phrases, images, allusions and so forth, to help students gain a full understanding of the text. They also raise questions or highlight particular issues or ideas which are important to consider when arriving at interpretations.

The fourth section, Interpretations, goes on to discuss a range of issues in more detail. This involves an examination of the influence of contextual factors as well as looking at such aspects as language and style, and various critical views or interpretations. A range of activities for students to carry out, together with discussions as to how these might be approached, are integrated into this section.

At the end of each volume there is a selection of Essay Questions, a Chronology, and a Further Reading list.

We hope you enjoy reading this text and working with these supporting materials, and wish you every success in your studies.

Steven Croft   *Series Editor*

Edward Thomas in Context

It was dawn on the 9 April 1917, Easter Monday. World War I, the so-called 'war to end all wars', had been raging for almost three years and the Allied forces were about to launch yet another assault on the German lines close to the French city of Arras, on the Western Front. For the past 20 days the allies had bombarded the German positions, but this was the day the Allied army would advance towards enemy lines. The morning was cold with sleet and snow in the air.

Second Lieutenant Philip Edward Thomas of the 244 Siege Battery of the Royal Artillery was on duty at his observation post. It was his seventieth day in France. Only the day before he had had a brush with death when a shell had landed very close to him, but it had failed to explode and his men had commented that he seemed to have luck on his side. At 5.30 am on the 9th an intense barrage had commenced along the 45 miles of the German front line and it was Thomas's job to direct the fire of his battery from his observation post at Achicourt. At shortly after 7.30 am a shell whistled by very close to him and exploded some distance away. Although he was not caught in the explosion the concussive blast from the shell killed him instantly, leaving his body completely unmarked. It was just a few weeks after his thirty-ninth birthday.

The early years

Edward Thomas was born the eldest of six sons on 3 March 1878, in Lambeth, London. Both his parents were Welsh and that sense of Welshness was important to him throughout his life. As a boy he frequently visited relatives in Wales and also Swindon, in rural Wiltshire, where he developed his life-long love of the countryside and the natural world. This also gave rise to the interest he developed in the work of Richard Jefferies, a Wiltshire writer noted for his depictions of nature and rural life. It was here in Wiltshire that, as a teenager, fishing on a riverbank, Thomas met David 'Dad' Uzzell. 'Dad', sometimes described as a 'reformed poacher', lived with his wife in Swindon but spent much of his time wandering the Wiltshire countryside and living his life free from the normal constraints of society. To Thomas he embodied the spirit of the free-roaming countryman who would later feature so often in his prose writing and eventually his poems, such as *Man and Dog* and *Lob*.

British infantry advance from a trench in the Battle of Arras on 9 April 1917 – the day Thomas was killed

When Edward was two years old, the Thomas family had moved to Wandsworth and he began school at the age of five at Wandsworth Board School, but his father moved him to a private school and a year later he won a place at Battersea Grammar School. In 1894 Thomas moved to St Paul's School, Hammersmith. Here he found things very different; it was an altogether more scholarly environment, and one in which he felt isolated and unnoticed. His father had hoped that he would thrive here and that it would help him on the road to a successful career in the civil service. The young Edward, though, proved a disappointment to his father when he failed to win the scholarship that would have significantly reduced the financial outlay needed to keep him at the school; the following year his father withdrew him.

However, while he was at St Paul's, his desire to write – which clashed so much with his father's desire for him to study for civil service exams – had led Thomas to write several essays based on the nature notes he kept. The minister of the chapel that the Thomas family attended read some of these and was so impressed with them that he showed them to James Ashcroft Noble, a former newspaper editor and a literary critic for several publications including *The Spectator*. After reading the essays Noble recognized something special in the young man's work, and he invited the 16-year-old to his home. There Thomas met Noble's three daughters; the middle one, Helen, was later to become his wife. Noble mentored Thomas and encouraged his literary aspirations, helping him to find a publisher for his first book, *The Woodland Life*, which was published when he was 18.

During this time Edward and Helen became close and spent much time in each other's company, often walking and talking together. After James Noble's death at the early age of 51 in April 1896, things became more difficult for Edward and Helen. Helen's mother had opposed their relationship from the outset and after her husband's death she forbade her daughter to meet with Thomas. Helen, however, refused to accept this and a serious breakdown in relations between mother and daughter culminated in Helen leaving home and taking a position as a governess for the Webb family in Broadstairs, Kent. Here she was responsible for looking after their young daughter, Hope.

Meanwhile, Thomas had won a scholarship to Lincoln College, Oxford to study history. It was clear by this time that he and Helen were lovers, but their refusal to marry further infuriated parents on both sides. They did find support from Thomas's old friend from Wiltshire, 'Dad' Uzzell and his wife 'Granny', with whom he and Helen briefly stayed before Thomas went up to Oxford. They were warmly received by the Uzzells, 'Granny' welcoming them 'as if we were her own children' and treating them as if they were a married couple.

In her memoirs, Helen Thomas recalls their feelings about marriage at this time:

> We had often spoken of our life together, and had made great plans for the education of our children. We hated the thought of a legal contract. We felt our love was all the bond that there ought to be, and that if that failed it was immoral to be together. We wanted our union to be free and spontaneous. We had no idea when it should take place, but the thought of our approaching separation heightened our desire to be united in body as we were in heart and spirit.
>
> (Helen Thomas, *As It Was*, page 42)

Thomas went up to Oxford in 1897 and Helen returned to London where she had secured another position as governess. In May 1899, during Thomas's second year at Oxford, Helen found she was pregnant and consequently was sacked from her position. Now the couple had to conform to convention, and they were married in June. The following January their son, Merfyn, was born. Lack of money, though, prevented them being together as a family and Helen had to move in with Edward's parents while he finished his degree. In this too he disappointed his father, achieving only a second-class degree and still shunning a career in the civil service.

A literary career

It is important to remember that by the time Thomas began writing poetry, 14 years after leaving university, he was a well-known writer of prose, a respected reviewer and an influential literary critic with a keen eye for poetry. He had more than 20 prose works to his name including travel writing, biography, a novel, and around 2,000 reviews, as well as innumerable pieces of writing that were unattributed.

One of the reasons for this huge output was his determination to support his family by writing. As much of his work was poorly paid and money was always short, he took on all the projects he was offered, and when there were no offers he went out and found more work for himself. This meant that he always had a huge workload, often involving work that needed to be completed to very tight deadlines. His writing may not have made him wealthy but it certainly earned him the respect of his peers, and he knew personally many of the key personalities of the literary world of the time.

However, leaving university with a wife and child to support meant that his early literary aspirations were quickly replaced by the constant need to write anything that would earn money. Often it must have felt to him that he was fighting a losing battle, as poverty was never very far away no matter how hard he worked. He and his wife began family life proper in a down-at-heel flat in a particularly poor part of London, but still he rejected his father's offer to help him find him a position in the civil service, and he refused to apply for possible teaching posts that might have been open to him. Instead, he contacted various literary editors and worked hard producing reviews for several papers. Still his income fell well below what he needed to support his family. After an unhappy few months in London he decided that a move to the countryside would give them a fresh start, and so the Thomas family moved to a rented house near Bearsted in Kent. The fresh start, though, never came. Thomas's poverty and despair increased. Soon after the move Helen became pregnant again and their daughter, Bronwen, was born in October 1902. At this time Thomas published a collection of essays, *Horae Solitariae*, and became close friends with the poet and verse dramatist Gordon Bottomley.

The combined pressures of the constant, unfulfilling writing, the ever-present worries about money and the turmoil of family life began to tell on Thomas and he started to suffer long bouts of depression, which in turn exerted an increasing strain on his relationship with Helen. Aware of what his dark moods were doing to his wife and family, he hated himself for it. He began going on long walks, often staying away for days at a time to spare them, and Helen became increasingly alone with her children.

In 1903, financial pressures were eased a little when he was offered £100 to write a book about Oxford for the publisher A.C. Black. Later that year the family moved again, this time to Ivy Cottage, also in Bearsted. However, both the book and their new home proved disappointments. *Oxford* had not brought Thomas any further reasonably paid work, and Ivy Cottage had proved insanitary: both Bronwen and Helen fell ill. The following year the family moved again, this time to a much more pleasant home at Elses Farm, near Sevenoaks in Kent. Helen fell in love with the place immediately and she enjoyed being in the midst of a working farm. Money worries and the pressure to earn enough to support his family still beset Thomas, but again commissions to write two further books, together with continued review work, saved them from poverty. Money worries eased at the expense of the increased pressure created by the non-stop stream of writing Thomas took on.

The years at Elses Farm brought some stability, and these were happier times for Helen and the children, although Thomas still felt the frustrations and pressures of his work. Helen recalls his feelings at this time:

> Edward had a fair amount of work, but never enough to keep
> him from anxiety, and never enough to free him from the
> hateful hack-work books written to the order of the publisher,
> which though he did them well did not at all satisfy his own
> creative impulse, the damming up of which contributed largely
> to his melancholy.
>
> *(World Without End*, page 106)

In 1906, the farmer retired and let Elses Farm. The new
tenants wanted the house that the Thomas family were renting,
and so they had to move again. Their next move was to Berryfield
Cottage, near the village of Steep in Hampshire, and Thomas
continued his punishing writing schedule. It was clear, however,
that the continual grind of this 'hack-work' was taking its toll on
him and his dark moods became more frequent and more intense.
Helen describes these moods when despair overtook him:

> the attacks of gloom and wretchedness had become more
> frequent of late and more lasting, and there were terrible days
> when I did not know where he was; or if he was at home, days
> of silence and brooding despair.
>
> *(World Without End*, page 113)

Anxiety about his depression and the effects of it on his
relationship with Helen prompted Thomas to visit a doctor to
seek advice about his 'melancholia', but little changed. Despite his
depressions, he continued to write continuously, and during these
years he produced some of his best prose works. In 1907 he was
invited to write a biography of Richard Jefferies, who had long been
a favourite of his, but even a commission such as this, because of
its tight deadlines and the pressure of other commitments, became
another task to be completed rather than a pleasure.

In order to find some peace and solitude to work on this book,
in the winter of 1907 Thomas left home for an indefinite period to
live in the borrowed cottage of a friend at Minsmere, Suffolk. While
in Suffolk he met the young girl, Hope Webb, who had been one
of the children Helen had looked after when she was a governess in

Broadstairs before they were married. Hope was now an attractive 17-year-old. She and Thomas became friends and frequently walked and talked together; he described their talks and meetings to Helen in his letters. Hope wrote to Helen too, and Helen became concerned that Hope was falling in love with Thomas; she warned her husband to be careful he did not hurt her. The infatuation came to an end when Hope confided her feelings to her older sister, who in turn immediately told their parents. Hope's father, who was very angry, told Thomas not to see or contact his daughter again, and in January Hope returned to her boarding school.

Soon after completing *Richard Jefferies* he was asked to write *The South Country*, a celebration of the English countryside and landscapes, its folk culture and natural history, inspired by travels through the southern counties of England. Despite the pressures under which they were written, both of these books were very well received and are regarded today as among the best of his prose work.

There followed, towards the end of 1909, another move: this time to Wick Green, overlooking Steep. It was here that their third child, Helen Myfanwy, was born in August 1910. The house was not a happy one for the family. In its high, exposed, hilltop position it was bleak and often windy and they found the atmosphere of the house oppressive. Money worries had returned as Thomas's review work had dried up, and he spent much of his time away in London trying to find more commissions or working on some unrewarding, unfulfilling task that paid little. Meanwhile Helen remained alone with the children, and when Thomas did return his depressions grew worse and worse. On top of everything, their baby girl became seriously ill and needed an operation. Although the baby made a full recovery, Thomas's health had become worse, his rejection of Helen and the family became more intense, and he even began to talk of suicide. In 1911 the combined effects of all this culminated in him having a serious breakdown. There was some improvement in his condition when he received treatment from a young doctor specializing in 'nervous disorders'; he continued to write throughout.

8

Edward Thomas photographed in London in 1912

Shortly before Christmas the following year, Thomas was introduced to Eleanor Farjeon, a young woman who was to become a close friend devoted to him and his work for the rest of his life, and who was to have an important influence on him. Andrew Motion (see Further Reading page 169) comments:

> Her cheerful company, and the undemanding love which she was to give, contributed enormously to the composure which made his poetry possible.
>
> (*The Poetry of Edward Thomas*, page 22)

There is little doubt that Farjeon came to love Thomas and he her, but it was a relationship that Helen approved of. In *World Without End*, Helen describes a conversation she had with Eleanor:

> If love could come to him again through you, Eleanor, it would
> be like a new heaven and a new earth. I should have my own
> sadness, but I should not grudge you his love, nor him yours,
> for I know that what is between Edward and me is eternal... If
> he could love you, Eleanor, I could not help but be the sharer,
> though how or why I cannot tell you – only I know it would be so.
> (*World Without End*, page 148)

In *Time and Again*, Helen puts it slightly differently: 'Edward was aware of Eleanor's devotion, but with the most sensitive tact kept it at a light-hearted level which she happily accepted' (page 93).

In the summer of 1913 the family moved to Yew Tree Cottage in the village of Steep itself. It was here that he finished several books he had been working on including *In Pursuit of Spring*, as well as continuing with some reviewing work. His depressions and irritable moods continued, and once again his marriage came under severe strain and he took temporary lodgings to remove himself from the family situation. In the autumn of that year, however, a meeting was to take place that would have a profound effect on Thomas and his future.

Thomas the poet

When he was in London Thomas regularly met, each week, a group of writer friends for tea at a London restaurant. It was at one of these meetings, on 4 October 1913, that the poet Ralph Hodgson introduced Thomas to the American poet, Robert Frost. There is no doubt that others had recognized the poetic potential of some of Thomas's prose writings, but the friendship that was to develop between himself and Frost over the next few months was to be a key influence in turning Thomas's desire to write poetry into reality.

Frost had come to England with his wife and family in the hope of finding a publisher for his poems and of meeting influential members of London literary society who might help him make a name for himself as a poet. He had brought with him many of his poems, which he intended to organize into volumes ready for publication. Frost had been introduced to fellow American poet Ezra Pound, and through him and other contacts he had met various other influential poets and writers, including Rupert Brooke, Robert Graves, Ford Madox Ford, Walter de la Mare and W.B. Yeats. Frost's eventual meeting with Thomas happened at St George's cafe in London, and marked the beginning of a friendship that was to have a major impact on both men.

By the time they met, Thomas was a respected figure in literary society as a critic and reviewer and Frost, four years his senior, was still seeking the literary recognition as a poet that had so far eluded him. Both had, in their own ways, experienced disappointments and felt despair, and both were still seeking their own kinds of fulfilment. Frost's first volume of poetry, *A Boy's Will*, had been published in April 1913 by the London publisher David Nutt. Frost was 39 and had at last had a volume of poetry published, but this moment of satisfaction was soon turned to disappointment by the lukewarm reception it received. Thomas, on the other hand, had a great desire to write poetry, something for himself and of himself that would give him fulfilment and lift him from the grind of his regular writing work, but doubted that this was something he would ever be capable of.

In May 1914 Frost's second book of poetry, *North of Boston*, was published and Thomas's very positive review of it, in which he described the poems as 'revolutionary', did much to draw attention to Frost's qualities and establish his reputation as a poet in both Britain and America. He and Frost found their views on poetry had much in common, particularly the belief that poetry should use the language of everyday life, capturing the voice and rhythms of authentic speech rather than using an unnecessarily elevated language that smacked of artificiality and insincerity. They also believed firmly that the true subjects of poetry would be found in the sights and sounds of nature and everyday life around them.

Robert Frost in England in 1913

In August 1914 the bond, both in personal friendship and the sharing of literary ideas, was cemented when Thomas and his family spent a holiday with the Frosts, who had rented a cottage at Leddington, near Ledbury, in Gloucestershire. The day after Thomas arrived at Leddington, Germany invaded Belgium and Britain declared war on Germany: the First World War had begun. As might be expected, this news caused a great stir in the country and the newspapers were full of jingoistic rhetoric; already the process of portraying all Germans as evil and all British as good had begun. Thomas hated this jingoistic talk and knew that nations of people could not be painted in such black and white terms. He was later to make his views clear in his poem '*This is no case of petty right and wrong*'.

After the initial impact of the news had passed, however, things began to settle down; the war seemed very distant from

Gloucestershire, and some normality returned, at least for the moment. Frost and Thomas spent many hours together walking in the Gloucestershire countryside talking of many things, but always their discussions returned to the nature of literature and poetry. Thomas became more and more convinced that rhetoric and formality often had a deadening effect on poetry. He was moving towards writing verse of his own.

On 2 September the Thomas family prepared to leave Gloucestershire to return to Steep. Thomas, however, did not return with his family, but took the train north to begin work on a commission for the *English Review* involving a series of articles based on the effect of the war on ordinary working people he met in different parts of the country. His travels raised his own awareness of the impact of the war and increasingly his thoughts turned to what his own response to it should be.

There can be little doubt that Frost's influence gave Thomas the strength and encouragement he needed to begin to write poetry. Frost had advised him that much of his prose work had poetic qualities to it, and could form the basis for poetry. In December 1914 Thomas completed the final draft of his first poem, *Up in the Wind* (see page 19). Over the next four days he completed a poem a day, following his first poem with *November Sky, March* (see page 22), *Old Man* (see page 23) and *The Signpost*, with another five completed that month. His close friend Eleanor Farjeon (see Further Reading) gave credit to Frost's role in this:

> In the Autumn of 1914 Edward's own living stream was undammed. The undamming was Robert's doing when, after reading his friend's prose, he told him he had been a poet all his life, and with plain talk for his tools started the water flowing... the poetry came down in a spate, and produced in Edward's being the enharmonic change that made him, not a different man, but the same man in another key.
>
> (*Edward Thomas: The Last Four Years*, page 55)

In evaluating Frost's influence it is important to acknowledge, as Andrew Motion observes, that 'Left to his own devices, it seems likely that Thomas would have started "trying to do something" in verse before long' (*The Poetry of Edward Thomas*, page 24), and Judy Kendall (in *Edward Thomas: The Origins of His Poetry*, see Further Reading) points to the influence of Thomas's other friends, such as Walter de la Mare, in encouraging him towards poetry. The outbreak of war no doubt introduced a further urgency, and all these factors combined to produce the sudden outpouring of verse that produced 144 poems over the next two years.

In autumn 1914 Thomas was busy preparing his anthology of writing about England, called *This England*. At a very late stage in preparation for publication in the autumn of 1915, it was found that two blank pages needed to be filled quickly. Thomas decided to include his own poems *Haymaking* and *The Manor Farm* under the pseudonym 'Edward Eastaway'; these were the first of his poems to appear in book form. (Another 18 of his poems, also under the name of Edward Eastaway, would appear in *An Anthology of New Poetry*, which was published in March 1917, just a month before Thomas was killed.)

As the war raged on, Thomas continued to work through his thoughts on it and to consider what his own course should be. The war had come close to home when Zeppelins bombed London, and there was a part of Thomas that felt the urge to enlist, as so many others had done. Frost, who had decided to return home early because of the war, had invited him to return to America with him. Thomas prevaricated; he felt torn between the attractive option of joining Frost in America and doing what he was beginning to see as his duty – joining the army to play his part in the war. By the time Frost returned to America in February 1915, taking Thomas's son Merfyn with him (he was to stay with a friend in New Hampshire), Thomas had still not decided what to do.

Finally, however, Thomas made his decision, and once made he kept to it unswervingly. On 13 July 1915 he enlisted as a private in the Artists' Rifles. What finally led him to make his choice is difficult to determine, but perhaps Andrew Motion comes as close as we can get to understanding it when he points to Thomas's own comment in his essay *This England*. Here Thomas examines his love for England and, through the outbreak of war, comes to the realization that 'it was not mine unless I were willing and prepared to die rather than leave it as Belgian women and old men and children had left their country'.

Having chosen his path, Thomas committed himself completely to carrying out his duties to the best of his ability. He continued to write poetry in his spare moments, and his experiences of military life provided him with some material, as can be seen in poems such as *Rain*, *Home* or *Lights Out* (see pages 57, 63 and 69). After initial training he was sent to Hare Hall Camp in Essex as a map-reading instructor and was promoted to lance-corporal and then corporal. In order to be closer to him, Helen and the family moved to High Beech in Epping Forest, and this also brought her closer to Merfyn, who had returned from America and was working in Walthamstow.

Thomas applied for a commission in the Royal Artillery, and after successfully completing his training as an officer cadet at the Royal Artillery School, in November 1916 he was commissioned as a second lieutenant. Although he had the opportunity to remain in England as an instructor, the following month he volunteered for service overseas. It is clear that by this stage he was determined to see action in France, and his posting to the 244 Siege Battery of the Royal Garrison Artillery ensured that this would happen.

Thomas arrived at Le Havre, France, on 30 January 1917, and was immediately assigned to a staff position at the battery headquarters. Again, he had the opportunity to avoid going to the front by continuing in his role at HQ, well behind the lines, but once again he rejected safety; he requested to be posted to frontline duties. By early February, he was finally at the front at Arras, carrying out his hazardous duties at his forward observation post, with the key task of directing fire for his battery. A few hours after the start of the battle on 9 April, he was dead.

In his last few months in England, Thomas had been able to spend time with Helen and the family. He had spent Christmas at High Beech with them, and over the weekend of 6 and 7 January, some of his friends came to say goodbye. One of these friends was Eleanor Farjeon. Thomas gave her instructions on supervising, together with John Freeman, the preparation of his poems for publication. This collection of Thomas's poems would be published in October 1917.

Eleanor left on 9 January, and a few days later Thomas and Helen parted for the last time. Edward had copied out all his poems into a book, which he gave to her before leaving for the station. Of all the poems he had written, he had seen only a handful in print. He did not live to see the volume of his poetry that would be published under his own name just a few months later.

Helen recorded that his final words to her were: 'Helen, Helen, Helen, remember that, whatever happens, all is well between us for ever and ever' (*World Without End*, page 172), and then he disappeared into the thick mist and snow.

After the battle: the ruined Place de la Gare in Arras, 21 April 1917

Selected Poems of
Edward Thomas

Up in the Wind

'I could wring the old thing's neck that put it there!
A public-house! it may be public for birds,
Squirrels and suchlike, ghosts of charcoal-burners
And highwaymen.' The wild girl laughed. 'But I
5 Hate it since I came back from Kennington.
I gave up a good place.' Her cockney accent
Made her and the house seem wilder by calling up –
Only to be subdued at once by wildness –
The idea of London there in that forest parlour,
10 Low and small among the towering beeches
And the one bulging butt that's like a font.

Her eyes flashed up; she shook her hair away
From eyes and mouth, as if to shriek again;
Then sighed back to her scrubbing. While I drank
15 I might have mused of coaches and highwaymen,
Charcoal-burners and life that loves the wild.
For who now used these roads except myself,
A market waggon every other Wednesday,
A solitary tramp, some very fresh one
20 Ignorant of these eleven houseless miles,
A motorist from a distance slowing down
To taste whatever luxury he can
In having North Downs clear behind, South clear before,
And being midway between two railway lines
25 Far out of sight or sound of them? There are
Some houses – down the by-lanes; and a few
Are visible – when their damsons are in bloom.
But the land is wild, and there's a spirit of wildness
Much older, crying when the stone-curlew yodels
30 His sea and mountain cry, high up in Spring.

He nests in fields where still the gorse is free as
When all was open and common. Common 'tis named
And calls itself, because the bracken and gorse
Still hold the hedge where plough and scythe have
    chased them.
35   Once on a time 'tis plain that the 'White Horse'
Stood merely on the border of a waste
Where horse or cart picked its own course afresh.
On all sides then, as now, paths ran to the inn;
And now a farm-track takes you from a gate.

40   Two roads cross, and not a house in sight
Except the 'White Horse' in this clump of beeches.
It hides from either road, a field's breadth back;
And it's the trees you see, and not the house,
Both near and far, when the clump's the highest thing
45   And homely too upon a far horizon
To one who knows there is an inn within.

''Twould have been different' the wild girl shrieked,
    'suppose
That widow had married another blacksmith and
Kept on the business. This parlour was the smithy.
50   If she had done, there might never have been an inn:
And I, in that case, might never have been born.
Years ago, when this was all a wood
And the smith had charcoal-burners for company,
A man from a beech-country in the shires
55   Came with an engine and a little boy
(To feed the engine) to cut up timber here.
It all happened years ago. The smith
Had died, his widow had set up an alehouse –
I could wring the old thing's neck for thinking of it.
60   Well, I suppose they fell in love, the widow

And my great-uncle that sawed up the timber:
Leastways they married. The little boy stayed on.
He was my father.' She thought she'd scrub again,
– 'I draw the ale, and he grows fat' she muttered –
65 But only studied the hollows in the bricks
And chose among her thoughts in stirring silence.
The clock ticked, and the big saucepan lid
Heaved as the cabbage bubbled, and the girl
Questioned the fire and spoke: 'My father, he
70 Took to the land. A mile of it is worth
A guinea; for by that time all the trees
Except those few about the house were gone.
That's all that's left of the forest unless you count
The bottoms of the charcoal-burners' fires –
75 We plough one up at times. Did you ever see
Our signboard?' No. The post and empty frame
I knew. Without them I could not have guessed
The low grey house and its one stack under trees
Was not a hermitage but a public-house.
80 'But can that empty frame be any use?
Now I should like to see a good white horse
Swing there, a really beautiful white horse,
Galloping one side, being painted on the other.'
'But would you like to hear it swing all night
85 And all day? All I ever had to thank
The wind for was for blowing the sign down.
Time after time it blew down and I could sleep.
At last they fixed it, and it took a thief
To move it, and we've never had another:
90 It's lying at the bottom of our pond.
But no one's moved the wood from off the hill
There at the back, although it makes a noise
When the wind blows, as if a train was running
The other side, a train that never stops

95   Or ends. And the linen crackles on the line
       Like a woodfire rising.' 'But if you had the sign
       You might draw company. What about Kennington?'
       She bent down to her scrubbing with 'Not me.
       Not back to Kennington. Here I was born,
100   And I've a notion on these windy nights
       Here I shall die. Perhaps I want to die here.
       I reckon I shall stay. But I do wish
       The road was nearer and the wind farther off,
       Or once now and then quite still, though when I die
105   I'd have it blowing that I might go with it
       Somewhere far off, where there are trees no more
       And I could wake and not know where I was
       Nor even wonder if they would roar again.
       Look at those calves.'

                         Between the open door
110   And the trees two calves were wading in the pond,
       Grazing the water here and there and thinking,
       Sipping and thinking, both happily, neither long.
       The water wrinkled, but they sipped and thought,
       As careless of the wind as it of us.
115   'Look at those calves. Hark at the trees again.'

March

Now I know that Spring will come again,
Perhaps tomorrow: however late I've patience
After this night following on such a day.

While still my temples ached from the cold burning
5   Of hail and wind, and still the primroses
    Torn by the hail were covered up in it,

The sun filled earth and heaven with a great light
And a tenderness, almost warmth, where the hail dripped,
As if the mighty sun wept tears of joy.
10 But 'twas too late for warmth. The sunset piled
Mountains on mountains of snow and ice in the west:
Somewhere among their folds the wind was lost,
And yet 'twas cold, and though I knew that Spring
Would come again, I knew it had not come,
15 That it was lost, too, in those mountains cold.
What did the thrushes know? Rain, snow, sleet, hail,
Had kept them quiet as the primroses.
They had but an hour to sing. On boughs they sang,
On gates, on ground; they sang while they changed perches
20 And while they fought, if they remembered to fight:
So earnest were they to pack into that hour
Their unwilling hoard of song before the moon
Grew brighter than the clouds. Then 'twas no time
For singing merely. So they could keep off silence
25 And night, they cared not what they sang or screamed,
Whether 'twas hoarse or sweet or fierce or soft,
And to me all was sweet: they could do no wrong.
Something they knew – I also, while they sang
And after. Not till night had half its stars
30 And never a cloud, was I aware of silence
Rich with all that riot of songs, a silence
Saying that Spring returns, perhaps tomorrow.

Old Man

Old Man, or Lad's-love, – in the name there's nothing
To one that knows not Lad's-love, or Old Man,
The hoar-green feathery herb, almost a tree,
Growing with rosemary and lavender.
5 Even to one that knows it well, the names

23

Half decorate, half perplex, the thing it is:
At least, what that is clings not to the names
In spite of time. And yet I like the names.

The herb itself I like not, but for certain
10   I love it, as some day the child will love it
Who plucks a feather from the door-side bush
Whenever she goes in or out of the house.
Often she waits there, snipping the tips and shrivelling
The shreds at last on to the path, perhaps
15   Thinking, perhaps of nothing, till she sniffs
Her fingers and runs off. The bush is still
But half as tall as she, though it is as old;
So well she clips it. Not a word she says;
And I can only wonder how much hereafter
20   She will remember, with that bitter scent,
Of garden rows, and ancient damson-trees
Topping a hedge, a bent path to a door,
A low thick bush beside the door, and me
Forbidding her to pick.

                              As for myself,
25   Where first I met the bitter scent is lost.
I, too, often shrivel the grey shreds,
Sniff them and think and sniff again and try
Once more to think what it is I am remembering,
Always in vain. I cannot like the scent,
30   Yet I would rather give up others more sweet,
With no meaning, than this bitter one.

I have mislaid the key. I sniff the spray
And think of nothing; I see and I hear nothing;
Yet seem, too, to be listening, lying in wait
35   For what I should, yet never can, remember:

No garden appears, no path, no hoar-green bush
Of Lad's-love, or Old Man, no child beside,
Neither father nor mother, nor any playmate;
Only an avenue, dark, nameless, without end.

The Other

The forest ended. Glad I was
To feel the light, and hear the hum
Of bees, and smell the drying grass
And the sweet mint, because I had come
5 To an end of forest, and because
Here was both road and inn, the sum
Of what's not forest. But 'twas here
They asked me if I did not pass
Yesterday this way? 'Not you? Queer.'
10 'Who then? and slept here?' I felt fear.

I learnt his road and, ere they were
Sure I was I, left the dark wood
Behind, kestrel and woodpecker,
The inn in the sun, the happy mood
15 When first I tasted sunlight there.
I travelled fast, in hopes I should
Outrun that other. What to do
When caught, I planned not. I pursued
To prove the likeness, and, if true,
20 To watch until myself I knew.

I tried the inns that evening
Of a long gabled high-street grey,
Of courts and outskirts, travelling
An eager but a weary way,

25   In vain. He was not there. Nothing
       Told me that ever till that day
       Had one like me entered those doors,
       Save once. That time I dared: 'You may
       Recall' – but never-foamless shores
30   Make better friends than those dull boors.

       Many and many a day like this
       Aimed at the unseen moving goal
       And nothing found but remedies
       For all desire. These made not whole;
35   They sowed a new desire, to kiss
       Desire's self beyond control,
       Desire of desire. And yet
       Life stayed on within my soul.
       One night in sheltering from the wet
40   I quite forgot I could forget.

       A customer, then the landlady
       Stared at me. With a kind of smile
       They hesitated awkwardly:
       Their silence gave me time for guile.
45   Had anyone called there like me,
       I asked. It was quite plain the wile
       Succeeded. For they poured out all.
       And that was naught. Less than a mile
       Beyond the inn, I could recall
50   He was like me in general.

       He had pleased them, but I less.
       I was more eager than before
       To find him out and to confess,
       To bore him and to let him bore.
55   I could not wait: children might guess

I had a purpose, something more
That made an answer indiscreet.
One girl's caution made me sore,
Too indignant even to greet
60   That other had we chanced to meet.

I sought then in solitude.
The wind had fallen with the night; as still
The roads lay as the ploughland rude,
Dark and naked, on the hill.
65   Had there been ever any feud
'Twixt earth and sky, a mighty will
Closed it: the crocketed dark trees,
A dark house, dark impossible
Cloud-towers, one star, one lamp, one peace
70   Held on an everlasting lease:

And all was earth's, or all was sky's;
No difference endured between
The two. A dog barked on a hidden rise;
A marshbird whistled high unseen;
75   The latest waking blackbird's cries
Perished upon the silence keen.
The last light filled a narrow firth
Among the clouds. I stood serene,
And with a solemn quiet mirth,
80   An old inhabitant of earth.

Once the name I gave to hours
Like this was melancholy, when
It was not happiness and powers
Coming like exiles home again,
85   And weakness quitting their bowers,
Smiled and enjoyed, far off from men,
Moments of everlastingness.

And fortunate my search was then
While what I sought, nevertheless,
90   That I was seeking, I did not guess.

That time was brief: once more at inn
And upon road I sought my man
Till once amid a tap-room's din
Loudly he asked for me, began
95   To speak, as if it had been a sin,
Of how I thought and dreamed and ran
After him thus, day after day:
He lived as one under a ban
For this: what had I got to say?
100   I said nothing. I slipped away.

And now I dare not follow after
Too close. I try to keep in sight,
Dreading his frown and worse his laughter.
I steal out of the wood to light;
105   I see the swift shoot from the rafter
By the inn door: ere I alight
I wait and hear the starlings wheeze
And nibble like ducks: I wait his flight.
He goes: I follow: no release
110   Until he ceases. Then I also shall cease.

The Manor Farm

The rock-like mud unfroze a little and rills
Ran and sparkled down each side of the road
Under the catkins wagging in the hedge.
But earth would have her sleep out, spite of the sun;
5   Nor did I value that thin gilding beam

More than a pretty February thing
Till I came down to the old Manor Farm,
And church and yew-tree opposite, in age
Its equals and in size. Small church, great yew,
10 And farmhouse slept in a Sunday silentness.
The air raised not a straw. The steep farm roof,
With tiles duskily glowing, entertained
The midday sun; and up and down the roof
White pigeons nestled. There was no sound but one.
15 Three cart-horses were looking over a gate
Drowsily through their forelocks, swishing their tails
Against a fly, a solitary fly.
The Winter's cheek flushed as if he had drained
Spring, Summer, and Autumn at a draught
20 And smiled quietly. But 'twas not Winter –
Rather a season of bliss unchangeable
Awakened from farm and church where it had lain
Safe under tile and thatch for ages since
This England, Old already, was called Merry.

The Combe

The Combe was ever dark, ancient and dark.
Its mouth is stopped with bramble, thorn, and briar;
And no one scrambles over the sliding chalk
By beech and yew and perishing juniper
5 Down the half precipices of its sides, with roots
And rabbit holes for steps. The sun of Winter,
The moon of Summer, and all the singing birds
Except the missel-thrush that loves juniper,
Are quite shut out. But far more ancient and dark
10 The Combe looks since they killed the badger there,

Dug him out and gave him to the hounds,
That most ancient Briton of English beasts.

The Hollow Wood

Out in the sun the goldfinch flits
Along the thistle-tops, flits and twits
Above the hollow wood
Where birds swim like fish –
5   Fish that laugh and shriek –
To and fro, far below
In the pale hollow wood.

Lichen, ivy, and moss
Keep evergreen the trees
10 That stand half-flayed and dying,
And the dead trees on their knees
In dog's-mercury, ivy, and moss:
And the bright twit of the goldfinch drops
Down there as he flits on thistle-tops.

The New Year

He was the one man I met up in the woods
That stormy New Year's morning; and at first sight,
Fifty yards off, I could not tell how much
Of the strange tripod was a man. His body,
5   Bowed horizontal, was supported equally
By legs at one end, by a rake at the other:
Thus he rested, far less like a man than

His wheel-barrow in profile was like a pig.
But when I saw it was an old man bent,
10 At the same moment came into my mind
The games at which boys bend thus, *High-cockolorum*,
Or *Fly-the-garter*, and *Leap-frog*. At the sound
Of footsteps he began to straighten himself;
His head rolled under his cape like a tortoise's;
15 He took an unlit pipe out of his mouth
Politely ere I wished him 'A Happy New Year',
And with his head cast upward sideways muttered –
So far as I could hear through the trees' roar –
'Happy New Year, and may it come fastish, too',
20 While I strode by and he turned to raking leaves.

Adlestrop

Yes, I remember Adlestrop –
The name, because one afternoon
Of heat the express-train drew up there
Unwontedly. It was late June.

5 The steam hissed. Someone cleared his throat.
No one left and no one came
On the bare platform. What I saw
Was Adlestrop – only the name

And willows, willow-herb, and grass,
10 And meadowsweet, and haycocks dry,
No whit less still and lonely fair
Than the high cloudlets in the sky.

And for that minute a blackbird sang
Close by, and round him, mistier,

15 Farther and farther, all the birds
    Of Oxfordshire and Gloucestershire.

Tears

It seems I have no tears left. They should have fallen –
Their ghosts, if tears have ghosts, did fall – that day
When twenty hounds streamed by me, not yet combed out
But still all equals in their rage of gladness
5 Upon the scent, made one, like a great dragon
In Blooming Meadow that bends towards the sun
And once bore hops: and on that other day
When I stepped out from the double-shadowed Tower
Into an April morning, stirring and sweet
10 And warm. Strange solitude was there and silence.
A mightier charm than any in the Tower
Possessed the courtyard. They were changing guard,
Soldiers in line, young English countrymen,
Fair-haired and ruddy, in white tunics. Drums
15 And fifes were playing 'The British Grenadiers'.
The men, the music piercing that solitude
And silence, told me truths I had not dreamed,
And have forgotten since their beauty passed.

Swedes

They have taken the gable from the roof of clay
On the long swede pile. They have let in the sun
To the white and gold and purple of curled fronds
Unsunned. It is a sight more tender-gorgeous
5 At the wood-corner where Winter moans and drips
Than when, in the Valley of the Tombs of Kings,

A boy crawls down into a Pharaoh's tomb
And, first of Christian men, beholds the mummy,
God and monkey, chariot and throne and vase,
10 Blue pottery, alabaster, and gold.

But dreamless long-dead Amen-hotep lies.
This is a dream of Winter, sweet as Spring.

The Unknown Bird

Three lovely notes he whistled, too soft to be heard
If others sang; but others never sang
In the great beech-wood all that May and June.
No one saw him: I alone could hear him
5 Though many listened. Was it but four years
Ago? or five? He never came again.
Oftenest when I heard him I was alone,
Nor could I ever make another hear.
La-la-la! he called, seeming far-off –
10 As if a cock crowed past the edge of the world,
As if the bird or I were in a dream.
Yet that he travelled through the trees and sometimes
Neared me, was plain, though somehow distant still
He sounded. All the proof is – I told men
What I had heard.

15   I never knew a voice,
Man, beast, or bird, better than this. I told
The naturalists; but neither had they heard
Anything like the notes that did so haunt me
I had them clear by heart and have them still.
20 Four years, or five, have made no difference. Then
As now that La-la-la! was bodiless sweet:

33

Sad more than joyful it was, if I must say
That it was one or other, but if sad
'Twas sad only with joy too, too far off
25 For me to taste it. But I cannot tell
If truly never anything but fair
The days were when he sang, as now they seem.
This surely I know, that I who listened then,
Happy sometimes, sometimes suffering
30 A heavy body and a heavy heart,
Now straightway, if I think of it, become
Light as that bird wandering beyond my shore.

The Mill-Pond

The sun blazed while the thunder yet
Added a boom:
A wagtail flickered bright over
The mill-pond's gloom:

5 Less than the cooing in the alder
Isles of the pool
Sounded the thunder through that plunge
Of waters cool.

Scared starlings on the aspen tip
10 Past the black mill
Outchattered the stream and the next roar
Far on the hill.

As my feet dangling teased the foam
That slid below
15 A girl came out. 'Take care!' she said –
Ages ago.

She startled me, standing quite close
Dressed all in white:
Ages ago I was angry till
20   She passed from sight.

Then the storm burst, and as I crouched
To shelter, how
Beautiful and kind, too, she seemed,
As she does now!

Man and Dog

''Twill take some getting.' 'Sir, I think 'twill so.'
The old man stared up at the mistletoe
That hung too high in the poplar's crest for plunder
Of any climber, though not for kissing under:
5   Then he went on against the north-east wind –
Straight but lame, leaning on a staff new-skinned,
Carrying a brolly, flag-basket, and old coat, –
Towards Alton, ten miles off. And he had not
Done less from Chilgrove where he pulled up docks.
10   'Twere best, if he had had 'a money-box',
To have waited there till the sheep cleared a field
For what a half-week's flint-picking would yield.
His mind was running on the work he had done
Since he left Christchurch in the New Forest, one
15   Spring in the 'seventies, – navvying on dock and line
From Southampton to Newcastle-on-Tyne, –
In 'seventy-four a year of soldiering
With the Berkshires, – hoeing and harvesting
In half the shires where corn and couch will grow.
20   His sons, three sons, were fighting, but the hoe
And reap-hook he liked, or anything to do with trees.

35

He fell once from a poplar tall as these:
The Flying Man they called him in hospital.
'If I flew now, to another world I'd fall.'
25   He laughed and whistled to the small brown bitch
With spots of blue that hunted in the ditch.
Her foxy Welsh grandfather must have paired
Beneath him. He kept sheep in Wales and scared
Strangers, I will warrant, with his pearl eye
30   And trick of shrinking off as he were shy,
Then following close in silence for – for what?
'No rabbit, never fear, she ever got,
Yet always hunts. Today she nearly had one:
She would and she wouldn't. 'Twas like that. The bad one!
35   She's not much use, but still she's company,
Though I'm not. She goes everywhere with me.
So Alton I must reach tonight somehow:
I'll get no shakedown with that bedfellow
From farmers. Many a man sleeps worse tonight
40   Than I shall.' 'In the trenches.' 'Yes, that's right.
But they'll be out of that – I hope they be –
This weather, marching after the enemy.'
'And so I hope. Good luck.' And there I nodded
'Good-night. You keep straight on.' Stiffly he plodded;
45   And at his heels the crisp leaves scurried fast,
And the leaf-coloured robin watched. They passed,
The robin till next day, the man for good.
Together in the twilight of the wood.

Beauty

What does it mean? Tired, angry, and ill at ease,
No man, woman, or child, alive could please
Me now. And yet I almost dare to laugh

Because I sit and frame an epitaph –
5 'Here lies all that no one loved of him
And that loved no one.' Then in a trice that whim
Has wearied. But, though I am like a river
At fall of evening while it seems that never
Has the sun lighted it or warmed it, while
10 Cross breezes cut the surface to a file,
This heart, some fraction of me, happily
Floats through the window even now to a tree
Down in the misting, dim-lit, quiet vale,
Not like a pewit that returns to wail
15 For something it has lost, but like a dove
That slants unswerving to its home and love.
There I find my rest, as through the dusk air
Flies what yet lives in me: Beauty is there.

The Gypsy

A fortnight before Christmas Gypsies were everywhere:
Vans were drawn up on wastes, women trailed to the fair.
'My gentleman,' said one, 'You've got a lucky face.'
'And you've a luckier,' I thought, 'if such a grace
5 And impudence in rags are lucky.' 'Give a penny
For the poor baby's sake.' 'Indeed I have not any
Unless you can give change for a sovereign, my dear.'
'Then just half a pipeful of tobacco can you spare?'
I gave it. With that much victory she laughed content.
10 I should have given more, but off and away she went
With her baby and her pink sham flowers to rejoin
The rest before I could translate to its proper coin
Gratitude for her grace. And I paid nothing then,
As I pay nothing now with the dipping of my pen
15 For her brother's music when he drummed the tambourine

And stamped his feet, which made the workmen passing
   grin,
While his mouth-organ changed to a rascally Bacchanal
   dance
'Over the hills and far away'. This and his glance
Outlasted all the fair, farmer and auctioneer,
Cheap-jack, balloon-man, drover with crooked stick,
20   and steer,
Pig, turkey, goose, and duck, Christmas Corpses to be.
Not even the kneeling ox had eyes like the Romany.
That night he peopled for me the hollow wooded land,
More dark and wild than stormiest heavens, that I
   searched and scanned
25 Like a ghost new-arrived. The gradations of the dark
Were like an underworld of death, but for the spark
In the Gypsy boy's black eyes as he played and stamped
   his tune,
'Over the hills and far away', and a crescent moon.

Parting

The Past is a strange land, most strange.
Wind blows not there, nor does rain fall:
If they do, they cannot hurt at all.
Men of all kinds as equals range

5 The soundless fields and streets of it.
Pleasure and pain there have no sting,
The perished self not suffering
That lacks all blood and nerve and wit,

And is in shadow-land a shade.
10 Remembered joy and misery

Bring joy to the joyous equally;
Both sadden the sad. So memory made

Parting today a double pain:
First because it was parting; next
15 Because the ill it ended vexed
And mocked me from the Past again,

Not as what had been remedied
Had I gone on, – not that, oh no!
But as itself no longer woe;
20 Sighs, angry word and look and deed

Being faded: rather a kind of bliss,
For there spiritualized it lay
In the perpetual yesterday
That naught can stir or stain, like this.

May 23

There never was a finer day,
And never will be while May is May, –
The third, and not the last of its kind;
But though fair and clear the two behind
5 Seemed pursued by tempests overpast;
And the morrow with fear that it could not last
Was spoiled. Today ere the stones were warm
Five minutes of thunderstorm
Dashed it with rain, as if to secure,
10 By one tear, its beauty the luck to endure.

At midday then along the lane
Old Jack Noman appeared again,

      Jaunty and old, crooked and tall,
      And stopped and grinned at me over the wall,
15   With a cowslip bunch in his button-hole
      And one in his cap. Who could say if his roll
      Came from flints in the road, the weather, or ale?
      He was welcome as the nightingale.
      Not an hour of the sun had been wasted on Jack.
20   'I've got my Indian complexion back'
      Said he. He was tanned like a harvester,
      Like his short clay pipe, like the leaf and bur
      That clung to his coat from last night's bed,
      Like the ploughland crumbling red.
25   Fairer flowers were none on the earth
      Than his cowslips wet with the dew of their birth,
      Or fresher leaves than the cress in his basket.
      'Where did they come from, Jack?' 'Don't ask it,
      And you'll be told no lies.' 'Very well:
30   Then I can't buy.' 'I don't want to sell.
      Take them and these flowers, too, free.
      Perhaps you have something to give me?
      Wait till next time. The better the day…
      The Lord couldn't make a better, I say;
35   If he could, he never has done.'
      So off went Jack with his roll-walk-run,
      Leaving his cresses from Oakshott rill
      And his cowslips from Wheatham hill.
      'Twas the first day that the midges bit;
40   But though they bit me, I was glad of it:
      Of the dust in my face, too, I was glad.
      Spring could do nothing to make me sad.
      Bluebells hid all the ruts in the copse.
      The elm seeds lay in the road like hops,
45   That fine day, May the twenty-third,
      The day Jack Noman disappeared.

The Owl

Downhill I came, hungry, and yet not starved;
Cold, yet had heat within me that was proof
Against the North wind; tired, yet so that rest
Had seemed the sweetest thing under a roof.

5 Then at the inn I had food, fire, and rest,
Knowing how hungry, cold, and tired was I.
All of the night was quite barred out except
An owl's cry, a most melancholy cry

Shaken out long and clear upon the hill,
10 No merry note, nor cause of merriment,
But one telling me plain what I escaped
And others could not, that night, as in I went.

And salted was my food, and my repose,
Salted and sobered, too, by the bird's voice
15 Speaking for all who lay under the stars,
Soldiers and poor, unable to rejoice.

'But these things also'

But these things also are Spring's –
On banks by the roadside the grass
Long-dead that is greyer now
Than all the Winter it was;

5 The shell of a little snail bleached
In the grass: chip of flint, and mite
Of chalk; and the small birds' dung
In splashes of purest white:

All the white things a man mistakes
10   For earliest violets
Who seeks through Winter's ruins
Something to pay Winter's debts,

While the North blows, and starling flocks
By chattering on and on
15   Keep their spirits up in the mist,
And Spring's here, Winter's not gone.

Lob

At hawthorn-time in Wiltshire travelling
In search of something chance would never bring,
An old man's face, by life and weather cut
And coloured, – rough, brown, sweet as any nut, –
5   A land face, sea-blue-eyed, – hung in my mind
When I had left him many a mile behind.
All he said was: 'Nobody can't stop 'ee. It's
A footpath, right enough. You see those bits
Of mounds – that's where they opened up the barrows
10   Sixty years since, while I was scaring sparrows.
They thought as there was something to find there,
But couldn't find it, by digging, anywhere.'

To turn back then and seek him, where was the use?
There were three Manningfords, – Abbots, Bohun, and
    Bruce:
15   And whether Alton, not Manningford, it was
My memory could not decide, because
There was both Alton Barnes and Alton Priors.
All had their churches, graveyards, farms, and byres,
Lurking to one side up the paths and lanes,

20 Seldom well seen except by aeroplanes;
  And when bells rang, or pigs squealed, or cocks crowed,
  Then only heard. Ages ago the road
  Approached. The people stood and looked and turned,
  Nor asked it to come nearer, nor yet learned
25 To move out there and dwell in all men's dust.
  And yet withal they shot the weathercock, just
  Because 'twas he crowed out of tune, they said:
  So now the copper weathercock is dead.
  If they had reaped their dandelions and sold
30 Them fairly, they could have afforded gold.

  Many years passed, and I went back again
  Among those villages, and looked for men
  Who might have known my ancient. He himself
  Had long been dead or laid upon the shelf,
35 I thought. One man I asked about him roared
  At my description: ''Tis old Bottlesford
  He means, Bill.' But another said: 'Of course,
  It was Jack Button up at the White Horse.
  He's dead, sir, these three years.' This lasted till
40 A girl proposed Walker of Walker's Hill,
  'Old Adam Walker. Adam's Point you'll see
  Marked on the maps.'

        'That was her roguery'
  The next man said. He was a squire's son
  Who loved wild bird and beast, and dog and gun
45 For killing them. He had loved them from his birth,
  One with another, as he loved the earth.
  'The man may be like Button, or Walker, or
  Like Bottlesford, that you want, but far more
  He sounds like one I saw when I was a child.
50 I could almost swear to him. The man was wild
  And wandered. His home was where he was free.

Everybody has met one such man as he.
Does he keep clear old paths that no one uses
But once a life-time when he loves or muses?
55 He is English as this gate, these flowers, this mire.
And when at eight years old Lob-lie-by-the-fire
Came in my books, this was the man I saw.
He has been in England as long as dove and daw,
Calling the wild cherry tree the merry tree,
60 The rose campion Bridget-in-her-bravery;
And in a tender mood he, as I guess,
Christened one flower Live-in-idleness,
And while he walked from Exeter to Leeds
One April called all cuckoo-flowers Milkmaids.
65 From him old herbal Gerard learnt, as a boy,
To name wild clematis the Traveller's-joy.
Our blackbirds sang no English till his ear
Told him they called his Jan Toy "Pretty dear".
(She was Jan Toy the Lucky, who, having lost
70 A shilling, and found a penny loaf, rejoiced.)
For reasons of his own to him the wren
Is Jenny Pooter. Before all other men
'Twas he first called the Hog's Back the Hog's Back.
That Mother Dunch's Buttocks should not lack
75 Their name was his care. He too could explain
Totteridge and Totterdown and Juggler's Lane:
He knows, if anyone. Why Tumbling Bay,
Inland in Kent, is called so, he might say.

'But little he says compared with what he does.
80 If ever a sage troubles him he will buzz
Like a beehive to conclude the tedious fray:
And the sage, who knows all languages, runs away.
Yet Lob has thirteen hundred names for a fool,
And though he never could spare time for school

85 To unteach what the fox so well expressed,
    On biting the cock's head off, – Quietness is best, –
    He can talk quite as well as anyone
    After his thinking is forgot and done.
    He first of all told someone else's wife,
90 For a farthing she'd skin a flint and spoil a knife
    Worth sixpence skinning it. She heard him speak:
    "She had a face as long as a wet week"
    Said he, telling the tale in after years.
    With blue smock and with gold rings in his ears,
95 Sometimes he is a pedlar, not too poor
    To keep his wit. This is tall Tom that bore
    The logs in, and with Shakespeare in the hall
    Once talked, when icicles hung by the wall.
    As Herne the Hunter he has known hard times.
100 On sleepless nights he made up weather rhymes
    Which others spoilt. And, Hob, being then his name,
    He kept the hog that thought the butcher came
    To bring his breakfast. "You thought wrong" said Hob.
    When there were kings in Kent this very Lob,
105 Whose sheep grew fat and he himself grew merry,
    Wedded the king's daughter of Canterbury;
    For he alone, unlike squire, lord, and king,
    Watched a night by her without slumbering;
    He kept both waking. When he was but a lad
110 He won a rich man's heiress, deaf, dumb, and sad,
    By rousing her to laugh at him. He carried
    His donkey on his back. So they were married.
    And while he was a little cobbler's boy
    He tricked the giant coming to destroy
115 Shrewsbury by flood. "And how far is it yet?"
    The giant asked in passing. "I forget;
    But see these shoes I've worn out on the road
    And we're not there yet." He emptied out his load

Of shoes. The giant sighed, and dropped from his spade
120   The earth for damming Severn, and thus made
The Wrekin hill; and little Ercall hill
Rose where the giant scraped his boots. While still
So young, our Jack was chief of Gotham's sages.
But long before he could have been wise, ages
125   Earlier than this, while he grew thick and strong
And ate his bacon, or, at times, sang a song
And merely smelt it, as Jack the giant-killer
He made a name. He, too, ground up the miller,
The Yorkshireman who ground men's bones for flour.

130   'Do you believe Jack dead before his hour?
Or that his name is Walker, or Bottlesford,
Or Button, a mere clown, or squire, or lord?
The man you saw, – Lob-lie-by-the-fire, Jack Cade,
Jack Smith, Jack Moon, poor Jack of every trade,
135   Young Jack, or old Jack, or Jack What-d'ye-call,
Jack-in-the-hedge, or Robin-run-by-the-wall,
Robin Hood, Ragged Robin, lazy Bob,
One of the lords of No Man's Land, good Lob, –
Although he was seen dying at Waterloo,
140   Hastings, Agincourt, and Sedgemoor, too, –
Lives yet. He never will admit he is dead
Till millers cease to grind men's bones for bread,
Not till our weathercock crows once again
And I remove my house out of the lane
145   On to the road.' With this he disappeared
In hazel and thorn tangled with old-man's-beard.
But one glimpse of his back, as there he stood,
Choosing his way, proved him of old Jack's blood,
Young Jack perhaps, and now a Wiltshireman
150   As he has oft been since his days began.

In Memoriam [Easter 1915]

The flowers left thick at nightfall in the wood
This Eastertide call into mind the men,
Now far from home, who, with their sweethearts,
    should
Have gathered them and will do never again.

Melancholy

The rain and wind, the rain and wind, raved endlessly.
On me the Summer storm, and fever, and melancholy
Wrought magic, so that if I feared the solitude
Far more I feared all company: too sharp, too rude,
5   Had been the wisest or the dearest human voice.
What I desired I knew not, but whate'er my choice
Vain it must be, I knew. Yet naught did my despair
But sweeten the strange sweetness, while through the
    wild air
All day long I heard a distant cuckoo calling
10 And, soft as dulcimers, sounds of near water falling,
And, softer, and remote as if in history,
Rumours of what had touched my friends, my foes, or me.

The Glory

The glory of the beauty of the morning, –
The cuckoo crying over the untouched dew;
The blackbird that has found it, and the dove
That tempts me on to something sweeter than love;
5   White clouds ranged even and fair as new-mown hay;

The heat, the stir, the sublime vacancy
Of sky and meadow and forest and my own heart: –
The glory invites me, yet it leaves me scorning
All I can ever do, all I can be,
10   Beside the lovely of motion, shape, and hue,
The happiness I fancy fit to dwell
In beauty's presence. Shall I now this day
Begin to seek as far as heaven, as hell,
Wisdom or strength to match this beauty, start
15   And tread the pale dust pitted with small dark drops,
In hope to find whatever it is I seek,
Hearkening to short-lived happy-seeming things
That we know naught of, in the hazel copse?
Or must I be content with discontent
20   As larks and swallows are perhaps with wings?
And shall I ask at the day's end once more
What beauty is, and what I can have meant
By happiness? And shall I let all go,
Glad, weary, or both? Or shall I perhaps know
25   That I was happy oft and oft before,
A while forgetting how I am fast pent,
How dreary-swift, with naught to travel to,
Is Time? I cannot bite the day to the core.

The Chalk Pit

'Is this the road that climbs above and bends
Round what was once a chalk pit: now it is
By accident an amphitheatre.
Some ash trees standing ankle-deep in brier
5   And bramble act the parts, and neither speak
Nor stir.' 'But see: they have fallen, every one,
And brier and bramble have grown over them.'

'That is the place. As usual no one is here.
Hardly can I imagine the drop of the axe,
10 And the smack that is like an echo, sounding here.'
'I do not understand.' 'Why, what I mean is
That I have seen the place two or three times
At most, and that its emptiness and silence
And stillness haunt me, as if just before
15 It was not empty, silent, still, but full
Of life of some kind, perhaps tragical.
Has anything unusual happened here?'

'Not that I know of. It is called the Dell.
They have not dug chalk here for a century.
20 That was the ash trees' age. But I will ask.'
'No. Do not. I prefer to make a tale,
Or better leave it like the end of a play,
Actors and audience and lights all gone;
For so it looks now. In my memory
25 Again and again I see it, strangely dark,
And vacant of a life but just withdrawn.
We have not seen the woodman with the axe.
Some ghost has left it now as we two came.'

'And yet you doubted if this were the road?'
30 'Well, sometimes I have thought of it and failed
To place it. No. And I am not quite sure,
Even now, this is it. For another place,
Real or painted, may have combined with it.
Or I myself a long way back in time…'
35 'Why, as to that, I used to meet a man –
I had forgotten, – searching for birds' nests
Along the road and in the chalk pit too.
The wren's hole was an eye that looked at him
For recognition. Every nest he knew.

40 He got a stiff neck, by looking this side or that,
Spring after spring, he told me, with his laugh, –
A sort of laugh. He was a visitor,
A man of forty, – smoked and strolled about.
At orts and crosses Pleasure and Pain had played
45 On his brown features; – I think both had lost; –
Mild and yet wild too. You may know the kind.
And once or twice a woman shared his walks,
A girl of twenty with a brown boy's face,
And hair brown as a thrush or as a nut,
50 Thick eyebrows, glinting eyes – ' 'You have said enough.
A pair, – free thought, free love, – I know the breed:
I shall not mix my fancies up with them.'
'You please yourself. I should prefer the truth
Or nothing. Here, in fact, is nothing at all
55 Except a silent place that once rang loud,
And trees and us – imperfect friends, we men
And trees since time began; and nevertheless
Between us still we breed a mystery.'

Words

Out of us all
That make rhymes,
Will you choose
Sometimes –
5 As the winds use
A crack in a wall
Or a drain,
Their joy or their pain
To whistle through –
10 Choose me,
You English words?

I know you:
You are light as dreams,
Tough as oak,
15 Precious as gold,
As poppies and corn,
Or an old cloak:
Sweet as our birds
To the ear,
20 As the burnet rose
In the heat
Of Midsummer:
Strange as the races
Of dead and unborn:
25 Strange and sweet
Equally,
And familiar,
To the eye,
As the dearest faces
30 That a man knows,
And as lost homes are:
But though older far
Than oldest yew, –
As our hills are, old, –
35 Worn new
Again and again;
Young as our streams
After rain:
And as dear
40 As the earth which you prove
That we love.

Make me content
With some sweetness
From Wales

45 Whose nightingales
Have no wings, –
From Wiltshire and Kent
And Herefordshire,
And the villages there, –
50 From the names, and the things
No less.

Let me sometimes dance
With you,
Or climb
55 Or stand perchance
In ecstasy,
Fixed and free
In a rhyme,
As poets do.

Under the Wood

When these old woods were young
The thrushes' ancestors
As sweetly sung
In the old years.

5 There was no garden here,
Apples nor mistletoe;
No children dear
Ran to and fro.

New then was this thatched cot,
10 But the keeper was old,
And he had not
Much lead or gold.

Most silent beech and yew:
As he went round about
15 The woods to view
Seldom he shot.

But now that he is gone
Out of most memories,
Still lingers on
20 A stoat of his,

But one, shrivelled and green,
And with no scent at all,
And barely seen
On this shed wall.

Haymaking

After night's thunder far away had rolled
The fiery day had a kernel sweet of cold,
And in the perfect blue the clouds uncurled,
Like the first gods before they made the world
5 And misery, swimming the stormless sea
In beauty and in divine gaiety.
The smooth white empty road was lightly strewn
With leaves – the holly's Autumn falls in June –
And fir cones standing stiff up in the heat.
10 The mill-foot water tumbled white and lit
With tossing crystals, happier than any crowd
Of children pouring out of school aloud.
And in the little thickets where a sleeper
For ever might lie lost, the nettle-creeper
15 And garden warbler sang unceasingly;
While over them shrill shrieked in his fierce glee

The swift with wings and tail as sharp and narrow
As if the bow had flown off with the arrow.
Only the scent of woodbine and hay new-mown
20 Travelled the road. In the field sloping down,
Park-like, to where its willows showed the brook,
Haymakers rested. The tosser lay forsook
Out in the sun; and the long waggon stood
Without its team; it seemed it never would
25 Move from the shadow of that single yew.
The team, as still, until their task was due,
Beside the labourers enjoyed the shade
That three squat oaks mid-field together made
Upon a circle of grass and weed uncut,
30 And on the hollow, once a chalk-pit, but
Now brimmed with nut and elder-flower so clean.
The men leaned on their rakes, about to begin,
But still. And all were silent. All was old,
This morning time, with a great age untold,
35 Older than Clare and Cowper, Morland and Crome,
Than, at the field's far edge, the farmer's home,
A white house crouched at the foot of a great tree.
Under the heavens that know not what years be
The men, the beasts, the trees, the implements
40 Uttered even what they will in times far hence –
All of us gone out of the reach of change –
Immortal in a picture of an old grange.

Aspens

All day and night, save winter, every weather,
Above the inn, the smithy, and the shop,
The aspens at the cross-roads talk together
Of rain, until their last leaves fall from the top.

5   Out of the blacksmith's cavern comes the ringing
     Of hammer, shoe, and anvil; out of the inn
     The clink, the hum, the roar, the random singing –
     The sounds that for these fifty years have been.

     The whisper of the aspens is not drowned,
10   And over lightless pane and footless road,
     Empty as sky, with every other sound
     Not ceasing, calls their ghosts from their abode,

     A silent smithy, a silent inn, nor fails
     In the bare moonlight or the thick-furred gloom,
15   In tempest or the night of nightingales,
     To turn the cross-roads to a ghostly room.

     And it would be the same were no house near.
     Over all sorts of weather, men, and times,
     Aspens must shake their leaves and men may hear
20   But need not listen, more than to my rhymes.

     Whatever wind blows, while they and I have leaves
     We cannot other than an aspen be
     That ceaselessly, unreasonably grieves,
     Or so men think who like a different tree.

Cock-Crow

     Out of the wood of thoughts that grows by night
     To be cut down by the sharp axe of light, –
     Out of the night, two cocks together crow,
     Cleaving the darkness with a silver blow:
5   And bright before my eyes twin trumpeters stand,

Heralds of splendour, one at either hand,
Each facing each as in a coat of arms:
The milkers lace their boots up at the farms.

'This is no case of petty right or wrong'

This is no case of petty right or wrong
That politicians or philosophers
Can judge. I hate not Germans, nor grow hot
With love of Englishmen, to please newspapers.
5 Beside my hate for one fat patriot
My hatred of the Kaiser is love true: –
A kind of god he is, banging a gong.
But I have not to choose between the two,
Or between justice and injustice. Dinned
10 With war and argument I read no more
Than in the storm smoking along the wind
Athwart the wood. Two witches' cauldrons roar.
From one the weather shall rise clear and gay;
Out of the other an England beautiful
15 And like her mother that died yesterday.
Little I know or care if, being dull,
I shall miss something that historians
Can rake out of the ashes when perchance
The phoenix broods serene above their ken.
20 But with the best and meanest Englishmen
I am one in crying, God save England, lest
We lose what never slaves and cattle blessed.
The ages made her that made us from the dust:
She is all we know and live by, and we trust
25 She is good and must endure, loving her so:
And as we love ourselves we hate her foe.

Rain

Rain, midnight rain, nothing but the wild rain
On this bleak hut, and solitude, and me
Remembering again that I shall die
And neither hear the rain nor give it thanks
5 For washing me cleaner than I have been
Since I was born into this solitude.
Blessed are the dead that the rain rains upon:
But here I pray that none whom once I loved
Is dying tonight or lying still awake
10 Solitary, listening to the rain,
Either in pain or thus in sympathy
Helpless among the living and the dead,
Like a cold water among broken reeds,
Myriads of broken reeds all still and stiff,
15 Like me who have no love which this wild rain
Has not dissolved except the love of death,
If love it be towards what is perfect and
Cannot, the tempest tells me, disappoint.

Roads

I love roads:
The goddesses that dwell
Far along invisible
Are my favourite gods.

5 Roads go on
While we forget, and are
Forgotten like a star
That shoots and is gone.

On this earth 'tis sure
10   We men have not made
Anything that doth fade
So soon, so long endure:

The hill road wet with rain
In the sun would not gleam
15   Like a winding stream
If we trod it not again.

They are lonely
While we sleep, lonelier
For lack of the traveller
20   Who is now a dream only.

From dawn's twilight
And all the clouds like sheep
On the mountains of sleep
They wind into the night.

25   The next turn may reveal
Heaven: upon the crest
The close pine clump, at rest
And black, may Hell conceal.

Often footsore, never
30   Yet of the road I weary,
Though long and steep and dreary
As it winds on for ever.

Helen of the roads,
The mountain ways of Wales
35   And the Mabinogion tales,
Is one of the true gods,

Abiding in the trees,
The threes and fours so wise,
The larger companies,
40   That by the roadside be,

And beneath the rafter
Else uninhabited
Excepting by the dead;
And it is her laughter

45   At morn and night I hear
When the thrush cock sings
Bright irrelevant things,
And when the chanticleer

Calls back to their own night
50   Troops that make loneliness
With their light footsteps' press,
As Helen's own are light.

Now all roads lead to France
And heavy is the tread
55   Of the living; but the dead
Returning lightly dance:

Whatever the road bring
To me or take from me,
They keep me company
60   With their pattering,

Crowding the solitude
Of the loops over the downs,
Hushing the roar of towns
And their brief multitude.

February Afternoon

Men heard this roar of parleying starlings, saw,
A thousand years ago even as now,
Black rooks with white gulls following the plough
So that the first are last until a caw
5   Commands that last are first again, – a law
Which was of old when one, like me, dreamed how
A thousand years might dust lie on his brow
Yet thus would birds do between hedge and shaw.

Time swims before me, making as a day
10   A thousand years, while the broad ploughland oak
Roars mill-like and men strike and bear the stroke
Of war as ever, audacious or resigned,
And God still sits aloft in the array
That we have wrought him, stone-deaf and stone-
        blind.

'No one so much as you'

No one so much as you
Loves this my clay,
Or would lament as you
Its dying day.

5   You know me through and through
Though I have not told,
And though with what you know
You are not bold.

None ever was so fair
10   As I thought you:

Not a word can I bear
Spoken against you.

All that I ever did
For you seemed coarse
15   Compared with what I hid
Nor put in force.

Scarce my eyes dare meet you
Lest they should prove
I but respond to you
20   And do not love.

We look and understand,
We cannot speak
Except in trifles and
Words the most weak.

25   I at the most accept
Your love, regretting
That is all: I have kept
A helpless fretting

That I could not return
30   All that you gave
And could not ever burn
With the love you have,

Till sometimes it did seem
Better it were
35   Never to see you more
Than linger here

With only gratitude
Instead of love –

A pine in solitude
40 Cradling a dove.

Celandine

Thinking of her had saddened me at first,
Until I saw the sun on the celandines lie
Redoubled, and she stood up like a flame,
A living thing, not what before I nursed,
5 The shadow I was growing to love almost,
The phantom, not the creature with bright eye
That I had thought never to see, once lost.

She found the celandines of February
Always before us all. Her nature and name
10 Were like those flowers, and now immediately
For a short swift eternity back she came,
Beautiful, happy, simply as when she wore
Her brightest bloom among the winter hues
Of all the world; and I was happy too,
15 Seeing the blossoms and the maiden who
Had seen them with me Februarys before,
Bending to them as in and out she trod
And laughed, with locks sweeping the mossy sod.

But this was a dream: the flowers were not true,
20 Until I stooped to pluck from the grass there
One of five petals and I smelt the juice
Which made me sigh, remembering she was no more,
Gone like a never perfectly recalled air.

'Home' [3]

Fair was the morning, fair our tempers, and
We had seen nothing fairer than that land,
Though strange, and the untrodden snow that made
Wild of the tame, casting out all that was
5   Not wild and rustic and old; and we were glad.

Fair too was afternoon, and first to pass
Were we that league of snow, next the north wind.

There was nothing to return for except need.
And yet we sang nor ever stopped for speed,
10   As we did often with the start behind.
Faster still strode we when we came in sight
Of the cold roofs where we must spend the night.

Happy we had not been there, nor could be,
Though we had tasted sleep and food and fellowship
Together long.
15   'How quick' to someone's lip
The word came, 'will the beaten horse run home.'

The word 'home' raised a smile in us all three,
And one repeated it, smiling just so
That all knew what he meant and none would say.
20   Between three countries far apart that lay
We were divided and looked strangely each
At the other, and we knew we were not friends
But fellows in a union that ends
With the necessity for it, as it ought.

25   Never a word was spoken, not a thought
Was thought, of what the look meant with the word

'Home' as we walked and watched the sunset blurred.
And then to me the word, only the word,
'Homesick', as it were playfully occurred:
30 No more. If I should ever more admit
Than the mere word I could not endure it
For a day longer: this captivity
Must somehow come to an end, else I should be
Another man, as often now I seem,
35 Or this life be only an evil dream.

Thaw

Over the land freckled with snow half-thawed
The speculating rooks at their nests cawed
And saw from elm-tops, delicate as flower of grass,
What we below could not see, Winter pass.

It Rains

It rains, and nothing stirs within the fence
Anywhere through the orchard's untrodden, dense
Forest of parsley. The great diamonds
Of rain on the grassblades there is none to break,
5 Or the fallen petals further down to shake.

And I am nearly as happy as possible
To search the wilderness in vain though well,
To think of two walking, kissing there,
Drenched, yet forgetting the kisses of the rain:
10 Sad, too, to think that never, never again,

Unless alone, so happy shall I walk
In the rain. When I turn away, on its fine stalk
Twilight has fined to naught, the parsley flower
Figures, suspended still and ghostly white,
15 The past hovering as it revisits the light.

'The sun used to shine'

The sun used to shine while we two walked
Slowly together, paused and started
Again, and sometimes mused, sometimes talked
As either pleased, and cheerfully parted

5 Each night. We never disagreed
Which gate to rest on. The to be
And the late past we gave small heed.
We turned from men or poetry

To rumours of the war remote
10 Only till both stood disinclined
For aught but the yellow flavorous coat
Of an apple wasps had undermined;

Or a sentry of dark betonies,
The stateliest of small flowers on earth,
15 At the forest verge; or crocuses
Pale purple as if they had their birth

In sunless Hades fields. The war
Came back to mind with the moonrise
Which soldiers in the east afar
20 Beheld then. Nevertheless, our eyes

Could as well imagine the Crusades
Or Caesar's battles. Everything
To faintness like those rumours fades –
Like the brook's water glittering

25 Under the moonlight – like those walks
Now – like us two that took them, and
The fallen apples, all the talks
And silences – like memory's sand

When the tide covers it late or soon,
30 And other men through other flowers
In those fields under the same moon
Go talking and have easy hours.

'As the team's head brass'

As the team's head brass flashed out on the turn
The lovers disappeared into the wood.
I sat among the boughs of the fallen elm
That strewed an angle of the fallow, and
5 Watched the plough narrowing a yellow square
Of charlock. Every time the horses turned
Instead of treading me down, the ploughman leaned
Upon the handles to say or ask a word,
About the weather, next about the war.
10 Scraping the share he faced towards the wood,
And screwed along the furrow till the brass flashed
Once more.
　　　　　The blizzard felled the elm whose crest
I sat in, by a woodpecker's round hole,
The ploughman said. 'When will they take it away?'
15 'When the war's over.' So the talk began –

One minute and an interval of ten,
A minute more and the same interval.
'Have you been out?' 'No.' 'And don't want to, perhaps?'
'If I could only come back again, I should.
20 I could spare an arm. I shouldn't want to lose
A leg. If I should lose my head, why, so,
I should want nothing more... Have many gone
From here?' 'Yes.' 'Many lost?' 'Yes, a good few.
Only two teams work on the farm this year.
25 One of my mates is dead. The second day
In France they killed him. It was back in March,
The very night of the blizzard, too. Now if
He had stayed here we should have moved the tree.'
'And I should not have sat here. Everything
30 Would have been different. For it would have been
Another world.' 'Ay, and a better, though
If we could see all all might seem good.' Then
The lovers came out of the wood again:
The horses started and for the last time
35 I watched the clods crumble and topple over
After the ploughshare and the stumbling team.

Bob's Lane

Women he liked, did shovel-bearded Bob,
Old Farmer Hayward of the Heath, but he
Loved horses. He himself was like a cob,
And leather-coloured. Also he loved a tree.

5 For the life in them he loved most living things,
But a tree chiefly. All along the lane
He planted elms where now the stormcock sings
That travellers hear from the slow-climbing train.

Till then the track had never had a name
10 For all its thicket and the nightingales
That should have earned it. No one was to blame.
To name a thing beloved man sometimes fails.

Many years since, Bob Hayward died, and now
None passes there because the mist and the rain
15 Out of the elms have turned the lane to slough
And gloom, the name alone survives, Bob's Lane.

Blenheim Oranges

Gone, gone again,
May, June, July,
And August gone,
Again gone by,

5 Not memorable
Save that I saw them go,
As past the empty quays
The rivers flow.

And now again,
10 In the harvest rain.
The Blenheim oranges
Fall grubby from the trees,

As when I was young –
And when the lost one was here –
15 And when the war began
To turn young men to dung.

Look at the old house,
Outmoded, dignified,

68

Dark and untenanted,
20 With grass growing instead

Of the footsteps of life,
The friendliness, the strife;
In its beds have lain
Youth, love, age and pain:

25 I am something like that;
Only I am not dead,
Still breathing and interested
In the house that is not dark: –

I am something like that:
30 Not one pane to reflect the sun,
For the schoolboys to throw at –
They have broken every one.

Lights Out

I have come to the borders of sleep,
The unfathomable deep
Forest, where all must lose
Their way, however straight
5 Or winding, soon or late;
They can not choose.

Many a road and track
That since the dawn's first crack
Up to the forest brink
10 Deceived the travellers,
Suddenly now blurs,
And in they sink.

Here love ends –
Despair, ambition ends;
15 All pleasure and all trouble,
Although most sweet or bitter,
Here ends, in sleep that is sweeter
Than tasks most noble.

There is not any book
20 Or face of dearest look
That I would not turn from now
To go into the unknown
I must enter, and leave, alone,
I know not how.

25 The tall forest towers:
Its cloudy foliage lowers
Ahead, shelf above shelf:
Its silence I hear and obey
That I may lose my way
30 And myself.

'Out in the dark over the snow'

Out in the dark over the snow
The fallow fawns invisible go
With the fallow doe;
And the winds blow
5 Fast as the stars are slow.

Stealthily the dark haunts round
And, when a lamp goes, without sound
At a swifter bound

Than the swiftest hound,
10 Arrives, and all else is drowned;

And I and star and wind and deer
Are in the dark together, – near,
Yet far, – and fear
Drums on my ear
15 In that sage company drear.

How weak and little is the light,
All the universe of sight,
Love and delight,
Before the might,
20 If you love it not, of night.

Notes

Up in the Wind

5 December 1914

Up in the Wind is Thomas's first poem and is based on a prose piece he had written a few days before, entitled *The White Horse*. The White Horse is an isolated inn (still in existence) situated high on the Froxfield plateau above Wick Green near Steep, and at 750 feet above sea level it is the highest inn in Hampshire. Thomas was a regular visitor to the inn and often sat in the bar writing ideas in his notebook. He finished a draft of the prose sketch on 16 November, but early in December, as Matthew Hollis puts it in his biography *Now All Roads Lead to France* (see Further Reading page 169), 'Thomas did something extraordinary that he had not systematically attempted in years. He began a poem.' The poem is a piece of verse-dialogue that tells the story of a young woman, the landlord's daughter, who had moved away to a new life in London, but who has returned to the inn and now serves ale to the customers.

1–4 **I could wring... And highwaymen** Note the use of direct speech to open the poem and establish the narrative voice.

5 **Kennington** a district of south London.

9 **forest parlour** The *parlour* is the 'tap-room' or public bar of the inn, which is surrounded by trees.

16 **Charcoal-burners** people who burn wood to make charcoal. Charcoal is used as a fuel for processes that require very high temperatures, such as in a blacksmith's forge. Charcoal-burners had been a feature of the English countryside for centuries.

27 **damsons** a fruit similar to a plum.

29 **stone-curlew** a bird noted for its distinctive loud, wailing cry.

32 **When all was open and common** This is a reference to past times when people had rights to common land for grazing and

agriculture, before the enclosures of the seventeenth century restricted land use to the landowners.

71–2 **all the trees… were gone**   i.e. they had been cut down for charcoal-burning.

75–9 **Did you ever see… a public-house**   The White Horse has no inn sign, just the empty frame that once held the sign.

March

5 December 1914

This is the third poem that Thomas wrote and was one of eight poems he sent to Robert Frost, who had been impressed with the poetic qualities of Thomas's prose works and had encouraged him to try using some of the material from his prose work *In Pursuit of Spring* (1914) as the basis for writing poetry. It seems likely, as Edna Longley observes (in *Edward Thomas: The Annotated Collected Poems*, see Further Reading), that Thomas uses elements of several March days he describes in *In Pursuit of Spring* to create his poem. In the poem Thomas anticipates the coming of spring as the weather on some days seems promising, but then reminds him that winter is still present.

1–3   The narrator's certainty that spring will come gives him the patience to wait for it.

4–9   Note the mixture of cold and warmth, reflecting the quickly changing weather of March.

11–15   Note Thomas's use of repetition in these lines.

18   **They had but an hour to sing**   The late appearance of the sun had stirred the thrushes to sing but they had little time before the sun went down.

28   **Something they knew – I also**   This links with the earlier question, *What did the thrushes know?* (16) – they instinctively 'know' that spring is near.

31   **Rich with all that riot of songs**   Some editions replace the word *Rich* with 'Stained'.

Old Man

6 December 1914

This is the fourth poem that Thomas wrote and, like *Up in the Wind* and *March*, it evolved from an earlier short piece of prose writing, this time one entitled *Old Man's Beard* that he had written the previous month. This prose piece was very short, only 300 words in length, and as Matthew Hollis comments, 'carried the feel of an accomplished prose poem'. Just a few weeks later he produced his first draft of *Old Man*.

The title of the poem refers to a flowering plant called southernwood, which was often used as a medicinal herb. The herb, which has a number of other names including 'old man', 'lad's love', and 'maid's ruin', gives off a smell that is not wholly pleasant. However, for Thomas, the scent of the herb held associations that sparked something in his memories. Thomas had a bush of old man growing by the door of Yew Tree Cottage at Steep, the third and last of his homes at Steep. On 11 November Thomas wrote in his notebook: 'Old Man scent, I smell again and again not really liking it but venerating it because it holds the secret of something very long ago which I feel it may someday recall, but have yet no idea what'. This note points us towards one of the concerns of the poem – smells can invoke memories of times long past. Thomas, though, is concerned with more than this and through the poem he explores what Andrew Motion describes as 'the effect that memory, children, scent and language have on his place in the natural world' (*The Poetry of Edward Thomas*, see Further Reading).

1–6 The names for the plant seem contradictory and do little to identify the thing they refer to.

  3 **hoar** white or silvery. The word is often associated with the white hair of old age. The combination in *hoar-green* adds to the contradictory description of the plant, as green is often associated with youth. This description, therefore, combines the ideas of youth and age.

4 **rosemary** a herb symbolically associated with remembrance.

9–10 **The herb... I love it** This is another paradox in the narrator's contradictory feelings towards the herb.

10 **child** Like the Romantic poets, Thomas presents the child as having a special kind of insight into the heart of things.

26–31 He is aware the scent stirs something in his memory, but what that is remains elusive, though too valuable to give up.

39 Normally the idea of an *avenue* suggests a road leading to somewhere, but here the words *dark*, *nameless* and *without end* present negative connotations. How do you respond to this final line?

The Other

December 1914

In *In Pursuit of Spring*, Thomas's account of a bicycle journey from London to the Quantock Hills in Somerset, he had written about a figure he called 'The Other Man' who had travelled with him for part of his journey. The poem *The Other* uses this idea of a fellow traveller but as a kind elusive double who is always ahead of the poet, and for whom the poet is mistaken as he pursues him through places that the 'Other' has left a short time before. In the poem Thomas draws on the symbolic significance of the 'double' in literature. The 'doppelganger' of folklore is often associated with sinister connotations, and there are similar associations to the double in various nineteenth-century novels such as Oscar Wilde's *The Picture of Dorian Gray* and Robert Louis Stevenson's *Dr Jekyll and Mr Hyde*.

1–7 **The forest ended... not forest** The narrator seems relieved to have left the isolation of the forest and returned to human habitation.

8–10 Note the sense of uncertainty created by the use of questions here.

10 **I felt fear** Note the introduction of this emotion here.

11–20 The narrator turns his back on the human company of the inn to pursue this *other*, in order to catch up with him and identify him.

24 Note the combined sense of being *eager* yet *weary*.

29–30 **but never-foamless shores... those dull boors** a dangerous shore with breaking waves would be more welcoming than those unintelligent and ill-mannered people.

31–2 He spent many days following his 'double', but never caught sight of him.

33–7 **And nothing found... Desire of desire** The narrator's sense of despair deepens and he finds nothing but the possible *remedies / For all desire* – Andrew Motion sees this as despair deepening to a suicidal level.

51 Note the distinction the narrator makes between himself and his double.

55 **children might guess** Thomas, like the Romantic poets, saw children as possessing an extra sensitivity and insight.

61–4 The narrator returns to a state of *solitude*. Note the repetition of *Dark* throughout this stanza. What effect do you think this repetition creates?

91–100 The emphasis shifts once more from solitude to society as the narrator continues his pursuit.

109–10 At last, the narrator recognizes he will never be without his 'other self'.

The Manor Farm

24 December 1914

The name 'Manor Farm' is traditionally given to a farm that was part of a manor in England. Under the manorial system dating back to the Middle Ages, the rural economy was organized into manors, each of which came under the power of the Lord of the Manor, the major landowner of the area. The agricultural produce of the Manor Farm was used to supply the needs of the manor. The name is still very common in rural areas of England, particularly in the south, and it has connotations of the archetypal English countryside of a bygone age. It is interesting to note that George Orwell used it as the name of the farm in his novel *Animal Farm* (1945). Thomas would have been very familiar with the name and its significance, and would know well the Manor Farm close to his home in Steep.

3   **catkins**   small flowers hanging in clusters or spikes, seen in early spring on trees such as willows, oaks and chestnuts.

5–6   The narrator is sceptical of the sun's power to signal the arrival of spring.

8   **yew-tree**   a coniferous evergreen tree often found in English churchyards. The yew is slow growing and very long-lived. There are many yew trees in England that are between 500 and 1000 years old.

11   **The air raised not a straw**   This observation emphasizes the tranquillity of the scene.

18   **The Winter's cheek flushed**   Note the personification that signals a change of style in the final section.

21   **a season of bliss unchangeable**   This reinforces the idyllic nature of the scene.

24   'Merry England' is a term often used to describe a utopian idea of an idyllic, pastoral way of life that supposedly existed in England between the Middle Ages and the Industrial Revolution.

The Combe

30 December 1914

A combe is a steep-sided, deep and narrow valley, often on a hillside, and combes are common features of the countryside of Hampshire. The setting of the poem is thought to be based on the narrow gorge of the Ashford stream close to Thomas's home in Steep. In the poem, the combe is the site of the killing of a badger, and it contains dark undertones that hark back to the land of ancient Britain.

1   **dark, ancient and dark**   The repetition emphasizes both darkness and the distant past.

2   **stopped**   blocked.

3 **sliding chalk**   loose, chalky soil. This is another feature of the chalk landscape of the area. The unstable chalk makes access to the combe difficult.

6–9 **The sun of Winter… quite shut out**   Both light and life are shut out of the combe.

8 **missel-thrush**   a large thrush that feeds on various kinds of berries. The bird's name is connected with mistletoe, which was held sacred by the Druids, the holy men of the Celtic tribes of ancient Britain.

10 **they killed the badger**   The reference to the killing of the badger gives the darkness of the combe a more sinister edge.

12   This line links the badger to the history of Britain, going back to ancient times.

The Hollow Wood

31 December 1914

The title suggests a wood in a hollow or dell into which (as with the combe, see above) the sun cannot penetrate, and where the trees are lifeless. In the poem, it is a place where the only symbol of life is the *goldfinch*.

1 **goldfinch**   a brightly coloured finch often seen feeding on thistles. The bird has often featured in religious art, and symbolically has associations with Christ. One legend has it that a goldfinch pulled thorns from the crown of thorns at Christ's crucifixion, and pierced its face, giving rise to the red patch around its beak.

3 **hollow wood**   Note the connotations of a dead place, empty of life.

4 **birds swim like fish**   How do you respond to this simile?

5   This line continues the unnatural imagery.

7 **pale hollow wood**   Note the repetition of *hollow wood*. This time the sense of a dead place is intensified by the modifier *pale*.

8   The narrator names three parasitic plants that grow in dark and damp places.

10 **flayed**   literally, stripped of skin. The term is often used to describe the result of whipping or lashing something.

11 **dead trees on their knees**   What is the effect of the personification here?
12 **dog's-mercury**   a highly poisonous woodland plant. The scent of this plant is foetid or foul smelling.

The New Year

1 January 1915

It has often been pointed out that several of Thomas's early poems use an approach very much in the tradition of William Wordsworth, in that they present narratives involving the meeting of solitary figures in wild or lonely places. In *The New Year*, the poet meets a man in the woods on a wild and stormy New Year's morning.

1–2 **He was the one man... New Year's morning**   The opening lines establish the sense of solitude.
3–8 Note the uncertainty, accentuated by the simile, as to whether he was a man or a beast.
11 *High-cockolorum*   a game involving bending and jumping.
12 *Fly-the-garter*   a version of the game leap-frog.
Leap-frog   a game involving one child bending over and another jumping over him.
14 What is the effect of this simile?
16 **ere**   before.
18 **the trees' roar**   This is a reminder of the storm mentioned in line 2.
19 See Interpretations pages 123–4.

Adlestrop

8 January 1915

One of Thomas's most famous poems, *Adlestrop* captures a short but timeless moment of tranquillity as a train makes an unscheduled stop at a sleepy country station. Adlestrop is a small village in the heart of the Cotswolds in Gloucestershire, near the market town of Stow-on-the-Wold. The inspiration for this poem was a journey that Thomas and his wife Helen had made travelling from London after they had attended a performance by the Russian ballet the previous day. On their way back from London they were visiting the Frosts in Ledbury, Hertfordshire, but the train made an unscheduled stop at Adlestrop. Thomas recorded the journey in his notebook.

4 **Unwontedly** unusually. The train did not usually stop at this station.

5 **steam hissed** Note the effects of the sibilance here.

6 The repetition of *no one* here emphasizes the sense of peace and emptiness.

10 **meadowsweet** a small flowering shrub, often growing in meadows.

haycocks conical mounds of hay collected together ready for gathering.

11 **No whit** not a bit.

Tears

8 January 1915

Thomas wrote this poem a few months after the outbreak of the First World War, at a time when he was reflecting deeply on the nature of war, and of England, and its impact on him. Michael Kirkham describes this period in Thomas's life as 'a process of troubled introspection that led a year later to his enlistment in the Artists' Rifles' (*The Imagination of Edward Thomas*, see Further Reading). In *Tears* he juxtaposes two apparently unconnected English scenes: one the traditional English fox hunt, and the other the changing of the guard at the Tower of London.

3 **twenty hounds streamed by me** The hunt presents a quintessential English image.

not yet combed out This perhaps suggests they were inexperienced or not fully prepared.

5 **made one, like a great dragon** What is the effect of this simile, do you think?

6 **Blooming Meadow** The Thomas family had lived at Elses Farm in Kent between 1904 and 1906. Helen Thomas wrote of the place: 'Of course hay-making on the lovely slope of Blooming meadow was a festival for us all' (*World Without End*, page 104).

8 **double-shadowed Tower** the Tower of London.

15 **'The British Grenadiers'** a very patriotic British marching song dating from the seventeenth century.

Swedes

15 January 1915

In this short poem, Thomas contrasts the life of nature against the idea of the afterlife.

1–4 **They have taken... Unsunned** Root vegetables such as swedes and turnips are often stored through the winter in piles covered with straw and earth. Here the farm workers have removed the end of the covering, letting the sun in on the vegetables.

4–10 **It is a sight... and gold** What is the effect of the comparison Thomas makes here?

11 **Amen-hotep** one of the pharaohs of ancient Egypt.

11–12 Note the use of antithesis here to contrast the *long-dead* pharaoh with cycles of the natural world.

The Unknown Bird

17 January 1915

Once again in this poem, Thomas takes as his starting point a memory from the past, this time the song of a bird he heard in a wood four or five years before. The Romantic poets such as Wordsworth, Shelley and Keats had all used birdsong as a muse or inspiration that provoked thoughts beyond the physical and led to an intangible world of the imagination.

   4 **I alone could hear him**   Note the sense of being alone that is introduced here and continued throughout the poem, and the suggestion that the bird was illusory.

  17 **naturalists**   Experts in the scientific world cannot help him discover the identity of the bird.

  18 **haunt**   What effect do you think this word creates here?

22–5 **Sad more than joyful… For me to taste it**   The repetition of *sad* here outweighs the sense of *joy*.

31–2 Perhaps the narrator is suggesting the bird acts as a kind of muse, to psychologically lift him to another plane.

The Mill-Pond

18 January 1915

Here Thomas recalls a moment of solitude beside the mill-pond as a storm approaches. He is angry when a girl startles him and warns him to take care. When the storm bursts, though, he realizes the wisdom and kindness of her advice. Some critics have interpreted this poem as containing a suggestion of the impact of the war.

   3 **wagtail**   a small bird often seen near streams.

   5 **alder**   a small tree of the birch family.

   9 **aspen**   a poplar tree.

16, 19 **Ages ago**   Note the repetition of this phrase.

  18 What is the effect of the girl being dressed *all in white*?

  24 What is the significance of the exclamation mark here?

Man and Dog

20 January

Like a number of Thomas's poems, *Man and Dog* focuses on a solitary individual. It is another example of Thomas using the experiences he wrote about in his notebooks to create poetry.

The poem describes a chance meeting with an old man and his old dog but, as Edna Longley observes:

> the primary focus is social history compressed into an individual life-story. The man's career as casual labourer spans rural and industrial work amid the advance of modernity and the advent of war. This time frame, however, also sits within a longer eco-historical narrative implied by his relation to the land.
> (*Edward Thomas: The Annotated Collected Poems*, page 185)

 2 **mistletoe**   a parasitic plant that grows by attaching itself to another plant or tree. It is commonly used as a Christmas decoration, but it has been highly venerated for centuries and it was, for example, a holy plant to the Celts.

 3 **poplars**   tall, narrow trees that grow to a great height.

 4 **for kissing under**   A popular custom at Christmas is to kiss under a sprig of mistletoe.

 7 **flag-basket**   basket made of reed.

 8 **Alton**   a village on the road from Chichester to Petersfield.

10 **'a money-box'**   savings.

15 **navvying**   hard physical labouring such as digging.

17 **'seventy-four**   i.e. 1874.

24 **another world**   i.e. the 'next world' or afterlife.

27–31 These lines describe the sheep dog, and its typical behaviour – often backing off and then closing swiftly in when possible to nip.

38 **shakedown**   makeshift bed, usually of straw.

39–42 **Many a man… after the enemy**   Note the references to the war and to soldiers in the trenches.

Beauty

21 January 1915

Thomas's bouts of depression are often referred to in Helen Thomas's writings. In *World Without End* she writes:

many of the days were saddened for us by Edward's anxiety,
and by that melancholy which had its roots in no material
circumstances, but came to cloud his spirit and our life, unbidden
and uncontrollable.

(*World Without End*, page 89)

This poem takes as its starting point one such bout of depression.

1   **What does it mean?**   Note the effect of the opening question,
creating a sense of puzzlement at his own state of mind.

7–9   **But, though I am... or warmed it**   The simile accentuates the
sense of gloom.

10   The metaphor gives a sense of harsh sharpness.

14   **pewit**   a wading bird also known as the lapwing or green
plover, which has a haunting, mournful call.

10–18   How does the mood change in the last nine lines of the poem?

15   **dove**   Doves are noted for returning unfailingly to their home.

The Gypsy

22 January 1915

Gypsies, with their nomadic lifestyle, their own traditions and
closed, secretive society have often been regarded as being outside
the mainstream society of England. In this poem Thomas's
perception of the gypsy woman combines a sense of both her
impudence (5) and her *grace* (4).

11   **sham**   false.

12   **translate to its proper coin**   turn into real payment.

14   **dipping of my pen**   i.e. writing (dipping his pen in ink).

17   **Bacchanal**   drunken or riotous. Bacchanalia were the wild
and mystical festivals of the Roman god of wine, Bacchus.

18   **'Over the hills and far away'**   a traditional English song
dating back to the late seventeenth century.

20   **Cheap-jack**   pedlar selling cheap goods.

21   **Christmas Corpses to be**   animals and birds to be slaughtered
for Christmas feasting.

22 **Romany**   another term for gypsy.
25–8 **The gradations... crescent moon**   Note the contrast between the images of death and life represented by the gypsy boy. The *crescent moon* is often seen as a symbol of fertility, life and re-birth.

Parting

11 February 1915

The parting referred to in this poem was between Thomas and his 15-year-old son Merfyn, who left the family home at Steep on 11 February 1915 with Robert Frost and his family as they returned to America. The relationship between Thomas and his son had often been a difficult one and their parting was strained. Matthew Hollis sums up the relationship:

> In fifteen years, Thomas had struggled to find a way to fully relate to his son. His own father had been pushily aspirational, and Edward would not make the same mistake with Mervyn [sic]; but he would make a different one, detaching himself to the point where his son was left uncertain of his father's feelings.
> (*Now All Roads Lead to France*, pages 207–8)

1–2 The past cannot be affected by what happens in the present. The first three stanzas go on to elaborate on this idea.
13–16 Pain is felt first of all through the act of parting and also through the fact that nothing can be done to change the situation that has developed.

May 23

15 February 1915

This is another poem that focuses on a character from a rural world of the past. Here Thomas presents a picture of the old tramp, Jack Noman.

12 **Old Jack Noman**   The character is based on a tramp who used to call at Thomas's house asking for old clothes and selling watercress (see line 27).

18 **nightingale**   a bird loved for its melodious song.

21 **harvester**   someone who harvests the crops, and so spends much time outdoors.

36 **roll-walk-run**   Note how the rhythm here captures a sense of his movement.

37, 38 **Oakshott rill, Wheatham hill**   *Oakshott rill* is a chalk stream where watercress grows abundantly. Both this stream and *Wheatham hill* are situated to the north of Steep.

39 The *midges* were brought out by the warmth of the sun.

46 What effect is created by this final line?

The Owl

24 February 1915

The narrator, hungry, cold and weary, seeks the shelter of an inn, where he finds food, warmth and rest. However, Thomas broadens this scene focused on personal needs to reflect on a wider realization prompted by the cry of an owl.

8–9 **melancholy cry / Shaken out**   Note the effect of the enjambment across a stanza break here, adding emphasis to the cry of the owl.

10 **No merry note**   The call of the owl is mournful.

13 **salted**   In what ways is Thomas's use of the word *salted* here ambiguous? Note its repetition in line 14.

'But these things also'

18 March 1915

In this poem Thomas observes the sights in detail as winter turns to spring. His observations, though, lead him to reflect on the fact that during this transition to spring, winter is not quite over.

3–8 The emphasis here is on the deadness of winter rather than the life of spring. Note the use of language evoking colourlessness.

16 What effect do you think the caesura (break in the middle of the line) has here?

Lob

3, 4 April 1915

This poem encapsulates several of Thomas's interests, including English folklore, place names and the traditions of the countryside. He explores his ideas through the character of the archetypal countryman, Lob. The name 'Lob' has several meanings: a country bumpkin, a clumsy, unsophisticated person, or a mischievous fairy. Here, though, Thomas uses the character of Lob to embody the idea of the old countryman deeply rooted in the countryside itself, a possessor of all the old knowledge of rural ways, and through his interaction with nature becoming a part of it.

9 **opened up the barrows** Barrows are ancient burial mounds. These are sometimes excavated by people in search of archaeological finds.

10 **while I was scaring sparrows** Children used to be paid to scare birds away from fields that had been sown with crops, to prevent them eating the seeds.

14 **Abbots, Bohun, and Bruce** three villages in Wiltshire collectively known as the Manningfords.

17 **Alton Barnes and Alton Priors** Alton is a parish in Wiltshire consisting of these two villages.

26 **they shot the weathercock** i.e. they behaved foolishly.

36 **Bottlesford** Another village in the area bears this name.

38 **White Horse** The shape of a horse had been cut into the turf of the hillside, exposing the white chalk underneath.

44 **wild bird and beast, and dog and gun** Hunting pursuits are in keeping with the position of the *squire's son*.

51 **where he was free** Note the emphasis on freedom.

52 The line suggests Lob is a universal, symbolic character.

60 **rose campion**   a flower whose common name is *Bridget-in-her-bravery*.

62 **Live-in-idleness**   another flower, perhaps the one often called 'love-in-idleness'.

64 **cuckoo-flowers**   also called *Milkmaids*.

65 **old herbal Gerard**   John Gerard (1545–1612) was an English herbalist and botanist noted for his book *Herball* (1597).

66 **Traveller's–joy**   Gerard so named this pretty flowering plant, because it grows along hedges and pathways by which people travelled.

68 **Jan Toy**   Lob's sweetheart.

73 **Hog's Back**   a ridge in the North Downs in Surrey running between Farnham and Guildford. A road runs along its length, part of the ancient ridgeway running from the Wiltshire Downs to the coast of Kent.

74 **Mother Dunch's Buttocks**   a local name for the Sinodun Hills in Berkshire.

76 These are places in Hertfordshire and Wiltshire.

80 **sage**   wise man.

90–91 **For a farthing... skinning it**   She would skin a flint or stone to earn a farthing (a quarter of an old penny) and ruin a knife worth sixpence in doing so. The term 'skinflint' is used for someone desperate to save money by any means.

98 **when icicles hung by the wall**   This is a reference to the song from the end of Shakespeare's *Love's Labour's Lost*.

99 **Herne the Hunter**   In English folklore, the ghost of Herne is said to haunt Windsor Park. Legend has it he appears with the horns of a stag on his head.

104–29 Here Thomas is drawing on tales from English folklore that involve marrying a princess, gaining wealth and vanquishing giants.

120 **Severn**   the longest river in Britain. *Shrewsbury* (115) is one of the towns it flows through.

121 **Wrekin hill, Ercall hill**   hills in Shropshire.

123 **Gotham's sages**   Gotham is a village in Nottinghamshire famed for stories telling of the stupidity of its inhabitants.

133 **Jack Cade**   leader of a popular revolt in the 1450 Kent rebellion against Henry VI.

136 These are local names for wild plants, as is *Ragged Robin* in the next line.

138 **No Man's Land**   originally wasteland, belonging to 'no man', but here the more modern reference is to the ground between the trenches of the opposing armies in the First World War.

139–40 **Waterloo, / Hastings, Agincourt, and Sedgemoor**   the names of famous battles in English history.

146 **old-man's-beard**   a plant also known as traveller's joy (see line 66).

In Memoriam [Easter 1915]

6 April 1915

This short poem presents a kind of memorial to the soldiers who had gone away to fight in a war from which many would never return. The flowers that should have been gathered by the men and *their sweethearts* lie unpicked in the woods. The poem is also a reminder that the war touches the lives of people far beyond those directly involved in the fighting.

1 **nightfall in the wood**   the sense of darkness created here is two-fold – the darkness of night and also the darkness within the wood itself. Thomas often used the wood as a symbol of darkness and isolation.

Melancholy

25 April 1915

Melancholy was one of the names that Thomas gave to the depression that troubled him at various times throughout his life. In this poem he captures a sense of the feelings of isolation that accompanied it.

1 Note the use of alliteration and repetition in this opening line. What effects do they create?

3 **Wrought**   created.

6–7 **What I desired... I knew**   How does this sentence sum up Thomas's dilemma?

8 **wild air**   This is a reference back to the *rain and wind* at the opening of the poem.

10 **dulcimers**   small stringed instruments played by plucking and strumming. They produce sweet, soft sounds.

The Glory

Early May 1915

This is another poem in which Thomas reflects on his feelings of lack of fulfilment. Here he begins by considering the beauty and glory of the morning as he observes the sights and sounds of nature around him. Even here, though, he feels keenly a sense of his own inadequacy.

1–7 The beauty of the morning is tempting him to feel happiness. Note how Thomas builds up the positive description line upon line here.

6 **sublime vacancy**   There is a feeling of uplifting happiness in the peace and emptiness of the scene.

8 **scorning**   rejecting or feeling disdain towards.

17 **Hearkening**   listening attentively.

19–20 His *discontent* seems as much a part of him as *wings* are a part of *larks and swallows*.

26 **fast pent**   held fast or trapped. The narrator feels trapped by his own nature.

27 **dreary-swift**   Note the paradox here, to reflect the narrator's conflicting feelings.

28 **I cannot bite the day to the core**   What do you think Thomas means in this final sentence?

The Chalk Pit

8 May 1915

In this poem Thomas creates two personas who hold a conversation, through which the key ideas of the poem are developed. One persona presents a realistic view of life while the other has a much more romanticized view. Both, though, are drawn to the deserted chalk pit. Some critics see the two voices of the poem as representing the two sides of Thomas himself.

3   **amphitheatre**   circular area of ground surrounded by higher ground. The word also means a purpose-built open-air arena for entertainment, as in the amphitheatres of Roman times.

4   **brier**   a generic name for various kinds of prickly plant such as brambles.

18   **Dell**   a small wooded hollow or valley.

44   **orts and crosses**   noughts and crosses. These lines suggest his face had become lined with the years of *Pleasure and Pain*.

53–4   **I should prefer the truth / Or nothing**   The realist prefers the unvarnished *truth*.

Words

26–28 June 1915

In this poem Thomas celebrates the importance and centrality of language to human existence. He writes of words as if they are living and powerful things. In writing about the poetry of John Clare, Thomas wrote that Clare:

> reminds us that words are alive, and not only alive but still half-wild and imperfectly domesticated... Words never consent to correspond exactly to any object unless, like scientific terms, they are killed... The magic of words is due to their living freely among things, and no man knows how they came together when a beautiful thing is made...
>
>   (*Feminine Influence on the Poets*, page 85)

5–9   Note the use of the simile here. What effect do you think it has?

13–14   **light as dreams / Tough as oak**   Thomas begins a series of similes here to show the scope and versatility of words and the association of words with the senses.

25–31 **Strange, familiar, lost**   Note the effect of the combination of these words.

33 **oldest yew**   The yew tree is extremely long-lived (see Note to line 8 of *The Manor Farm*, page 78).

35 **Worn new**   Note the oxymoron.

40–41 **the earth which you prove / That we love**   The words we use to express ourselves are part of the world, part of us – names and things are inextricably linked. (See *Old Man*, page 23.)

43–4 **some sweetness / From Wales**   Note Thomas's feeling of the therapeutic properties of Wales.

45–6 The habitat of the nightingale does not extend into Wales.

57–8 What do you think is the effect of this final paradox?

Under the Wood

5 July 1915

Thomas again here sets the transience of human existence against the background of the natural world. The poet reflects on the old gamekeeper, now gone, and his deserted cottage; the only sign that he was ever there is the shrivelled green carcass of a stoat he once shot. Now, all is deserted and seems insignificant against the surrounding trees.

5–8 This stanza describes things suggestive of life and growth.

6 **mistletoe**   Mention of this plant brings to mind the Christmas tradition of kissing under it (see Notes to *Man and Dog* lines 2 and 4, page 84). The old keeper had lived alone.

9 **cot**   cottage.

13 **beech and yew**   Both of these types of tree are extremely long-lived.

16 A gamekeeper would normally shoot creatures that were considered pests.

17–24 The gamekeeper is now gone and forgotten, and the only thing remaining to show he was ever there is the old *shrivelled* carcass of a stoat fastened to the *shed wall*.

20 **stoat**   small, fierce, ferret-like animal often killed by gamekeepers, as they are a threat to game birds.

93

Haymaking

6–8 July 1915

Haymaking, together with *The Manor Farm*, was first published in an anthology of poems Thomas had edited called *This England*. As described on page 14, his contribution arose after the publisher asked him to fill two blank pages that remained after the material had been typeset. He decided to fill the space by including his own poems, *The Manor Farm* and *Haymaking*, under the name of Edward Eastaway. Through this chance occurrence, the two poems became his first to be published in book form.

In *Haymaking*, Thomas captures a scene of the English pastoral landscape as farm labourers gather the hay.

1–6	Note the description of the weather setting the atmosphere for the poem.
2	**kernel** grain or seed (used here metaphorically).
14	**nettle-creeper** colloquial name for the whitethroat, a species of warbler. The bird is so called because of its habit of searching for food under overgrown hedges.
17–18	The simile captures the bow-like shape of the swift's wings in flight.
19	**woodbine** honeysuckle, a climbing plant that gives off a sweet scent.
22	**Haymakers** the labourers who gather in the hay.
24	**Without its team** The team of horses that pull the hay-cart had been unharnessed.
33–4	What effect do you think these lines create?
35	**Clare and Cowper, Morland and Crome** The poets John Clare (1793–1864) and William Cowper (1731–1800) are noted for their poetry describing scenes of nature and everyday country life; George Morland (1763–1804) and John Crome (1768–1821) were artists famous for their paintings of the English countryside and rustic scenes.
42	**grange** farmhouse with farm buildings.

Aspens

11 July 1915

When Thomas wrote *Aspens* in July 1915 he sent a copy to Robert Frost immediately, together with a letter explaining that he had enlisted in the army. Frost described this poem as 'the loveliest of all'. Often, tall-growing aspen trees were planted close to settlements or houses on the side of the prevailing wind, to offer the habitation some protection against the weather. In the poem Thomas identifies himself with the trees.

   2   **the inn, the smithy, and the shop**   These were the key elements at the heart of a community.

   3   **aspens**   tall, slender trees with small leaves that tremble even in the slightest breeze, producing a whispering sound.

5–8   Note the link created between the *blacksmith's* and the *inn*.

   5   **the blacksmith's cavern**   What effect does Thomas achieve by describing the blacksmith's forge as a *cavern*?

  10   **lightless pane and footless road**   The place is now emptied of its inhabitants.

  15   **the night of nightingales**   The nightingale's song is usually heard on calm and tranquil nights.

21–4   **while they and I... like a different tree**   Thomas completes his identification with the aspens.

Cock-Crow

23 July 1915

This was the fourth poem that Thomas wrote after joining the army, and at this time thoughts of the conflict that was raging in France and his future role in it were very much in his mind. Some have thought of this poem as a kind of 'call to arms'. In it, Thomas describes awakening at dawn to the sound of a cock crowing, but his use of language makes the link to military life and the call of the bugle very clear.

1 **Out of the wood of thoughts**   Note here Thomas's use of
 one of his favourite images to convey a sense of darkness.

2 The metaphor is extended.

5–6 **And bright... Heralds of splendour**   Note the transition
 from *two cocks together crow* (line 3)

8 The final line returns us to the pastoral scene as the farm
 workers prepare to milk the cows.

'This is no case of petty right or wrong'

26 December 1915

At the heart of this poem are Thomas's thoughts and views about
the war and patriotism. Since the outbreak of war on 4 August
1914, Thomas had been working through in his mind his responses
and feelings towards the situation. Eventually, after much soul-
searching, in July 1915 he enlisted in the Artists' Rifles. A number
of critics have pointed to the biographical evidence that indicates
this poem was written as a reaction against those who held a very
zealous, jingoistic attitude towards the war. Although much of his
poetry suggests Thomas had a deep love of England and was a true
patriot, as Eleanor Farjeon tells us (in *Edward Thomas: The Last
Four Years*, see Further Reading), he hated 'the jingo press and those
who used its jargon in argument. His father was amongst them'.
Andrew Motion also points to the disagreement between Thomas
and his father recounted in a letter he wrote to Frost describing his
father during the Christmas period in which he wrote the poem.

1–3 **This is no case... Can judge**   Note the irony of these
 opening lines, suggesting that *politicians or philosophers* can
 make judgements on trivial issues, but this is too important
 for them to judge.

4 **to please newspapers**   Thomas despised the jingoism of
 some newspapers. He refused to hate Germans or become
 blind with the kind of patriotism pumped out by many
 newspapers of the time.

12 **Athwart**   across, moving from one side to the other.
12–15 **Two witches... died yesterday**   The narrator hopes for a
post-war England that is like the one before the war.
16–19 The narrator is not interested in the historical / political
analysis of war.
22 **what never slaves and cattle blessed**   i.e. the tradition of
English liberty.

Rain

7 January 1916

Rain is a central symbol in Thomas's poetry, and he uses it to
express various qualities, sometimes contradictory ones. His
differing attitudes, both positive and negative, towards rain can be
seen in his some of prose writings. Although Thomas wrote this
poem at Hare Hall Camp and the *bleak hut* (2) is his army billet,
Matthew Hollis indicates that he drew heavily on the torrential
rain he had experienced on the Icknield Way, where he wrote of
the rain as a destructive force:

> The rain has drowned the splendour. Everything is drowned
> and dead, all that was once lovely and alive in the world, all
> that had once been alive and memorable though dead is now
> dung for a future that is infinitely less than the falling dark
> rain.
>
> (*The Icknield Way*, page 282)

Although in *Rain* he does not overtly mention the war, he
contemplates death and its inevitability.

2 **this bleak hut**   an army hut at Hare Hall Camp.
5 **washing me cleaner**   The rain seems to both add to his
despair and wash him clean.
7–9 **Blessed are the dead... dying tonight**   These lines are
suggestive of the dead and dying soldiers.
14 **Myriads**   a very large number (referring here to the huge
numbers of war dead).

Roads

22 January 1916

The idea and imagery of roads is of central importance in many of Thomas's poems. Many of his poems refer to roads and journeys, and descriptions of travellers appear time and time again. He opens *The Icknield Way* with some reflections on the nature of roads:

> Much has been written of travel, far less of the road. Writers have treated the road as a passive means to an end... they leave the impression that a road is a connection between two points which only exists when the traveller is upon it... Yet to a nomadic people the road was as important as anything upon it... It is a silent companion always ready for us, whether it be day or night, wet or fine, whether we are calm or desperate, well or sick. It is always going: it is never gone right away, and no man is too late.
>
> (*The Icknield Way*, pages 1–2)

In this poem, Thomas reflects on the significance of roads, exploring their nature, the gods that are associated with them, and how ultimately, for him, they all lead to France.

25–8   Several critics have pointed to the reminder here of John Bunyan's *The Pilgrim's Progress*, an allegorical poem written in the seventeenth century which tells of the journey of Christian, the central character, to the 'Celestial City' or heaven.

33   Helen's story is told in the *Mabinogion* (see line 35), a collection of medieval Welsh tales. She was married to the Emperor Maxen, and she persuaded her husband to build roads to connect the strongholds throughout the kingdom so that soldiers could move about more easily to defend it from attack.

48   **chanticleer**   name for a cockerel that appears in several medieval stories, including Geoffrey Chaucer's *The Nun's Priest's Tale*. In the tale Chanticleer dreams of his own death, being killed by the fox. Here, the cock-crow brings the dawn.

February Afternoon

7, 8 February 1916

Thomas wrote six sonnets in his short life as a poet, and in *February Afternoon*, his second, once again his focus is on the war, which he sees as representative of all wars of the past.

1 **parleying starlings**   Thomas had previously noted starlings chattering together in the trees and hedges. However, coupling the description of them here with the word *parleying*, with its connotations of a discussion between opposing sides in a conflict, suggests the idea of war.

2 **A thousand years ago**   Note the way that Thomas gives the poem a historical perspective.

4–5 **first are last... last are first**   'But many that are first shall be last; and the last shall be first' (Matthew 19:30). What effect does this biblical reference have on the poem?

8 **shaw**   archaic term for a small wood or copse.

10–11 **broad ploughland oak / Roars mill-like**   The metaphor encompasses both the natural and the industrial world.

13–14 God seems *deaf* and *blind* to the horrors and suffering of war.

'No one so much as you'

11 February 1916

This is one of several 'love' poems Thomas wrote in 1916. There is some debate about who the poem is addressed to, and some critics cite evidence that indicates it is addressed to Thomas's mother. Others, though, believe that the poem is addressed to his wife Helen. In his biography of Thomas, Matthew Hollis explores this question and concludes:

> The love poems he wrote in the winter of 1916 do not point neatly to one person; nor should it be assumed that their author was in love in order to have written them (he had

stressed that he was not)... Thomas had been at pains to tell Helen that he was in fact incapable of loving.

(*Now All Roads Lead to France*, page 268)

1, 3 **as you** Note the repetition here. What effect does it create?

Celandine

4 March 1916

This poem centres around Thomas's memory of a young girl, and explores how memory can distort the truth and create its own kind of fantasy of past events. Ultimately Thomas rejects the romanticized memory in favour of reality.

9–10 **Her nature and name / Were like those flowers** Some have suggested that Hope Webb (see pages 7–8) is the girl in the poem. As Edna Longley comments on these lines, '"Hope" would fit the bill' here (*Edward Thomas: The Annotated Collected Poems*, page 281).

11 **short swift eternity** Note the use of the oxymoron here. What is its effect?

18 **locks sweeping the mossy sod** Longley (see Note to lines 9–10) notes that accounts of Hope stress her long hair.

23 **air** tune, melody or song.

Home [3]

7 and 10 March 1916

Thomas wrote three poems entitled *Home* in which he describes his time at Hare Hall Camp in the spring of 1916. During this time he was becoming increasingly restless, a feeling exacerbated because, as Matthew Hollis puts it, 'He could neither see an end to the conflict nor very clearly what his role would be' (*Now All Roads Lead to France*, page 273). Thomas did, however, get some chance to walk in the surrounding countryside and the poem describes his return to camp from one of these walks accompanied by two of his comrades.

   8 The camp had nothing to draw them back to it except the
       necessity to return.
  12 **cold roofs** This has the suggestion of being cold in more
       senses than simply the physical; the place was strange and
       lacking in spiritual warmth.
  14 **fellowship** comradeship (among the soldiers).
  17 Why do you think the word made them smile?
20–24 The men were drawn from different areas and were not friends
       in the normal sense, but were united by a common bond
       forged from the circumstances they found themselves in.
28–35 What does Thomas reveal about his own feelings in these final
       lines of the poem?

Thaw

10 March 1916

Thaw continues in the same setting as *Home* and presents, as Edna Longley puts it, 'an upbeat coda' or concluding section to it (*Edward Thomas: The Annotated Collected Poems*, page 284). The mood here is much more positive, as the snow is thawing and signs of new life are emerging as the rooks start to nest.

   2 **speculating** Why do you think Thomas uses the word here?
       What effect does it create?

It Rains

11–13 May 1916

Rain is an important symbol in Thomas's poetry and it appears frequently in his writings, both prose and poetry. In *The South Country* he had written: 'In its noise and myriad aspects I feel the mortal beauty of immortal things' (*The South Country*, page 234). In *It Rains*, Thomas reflects on the loss of love but also the past happiness that love brought.

> 1–5 Note the sense of absence created in this stanza.
>   3 **Forest of parsley** Parsley is a large weed with white flowers found in hedgerows and uncultivated ground.
>   10 **never, never again** Note the use of repetition here.
>   13 **fined to naught** The deepening *Twilight* has made it impossible to see the stalks of the parsley flowers, so it appears that the *white* blooms are *suspended* in the air.

'The sun used to shine'

22 May 1916

In this poem Thomas looks back to the time he spent with Robert Frost and the friendship that grew up between them in the summer of 1914, the summer that war broke out. During the time they spent together, the two often walked in the Gloucestershire countryside talking and looking at the natural world together. At this stage the war seems *remote* (9), and intrudes little into their pastoral world. However, as the moon rises, thoughts of the war begin to grow.

>   13 **sentry of dark betonies** Betonies are flowers often found on the edges of woodland. Note here the use of the word *sentry* and the military connotations it introduces.
>   17 **Hades** the underworld, the realm of the dead, in Greek mythology.
>   21 **Crusades** a series of religious wars between Christians and Muslims that took place from the eleventh to the thirteenth centuries.
>   22 **Caesar's battles** Julius Caesar was a Roman general and successful military commander.

'As the team's head brass'

27 May 1916

This is another poem Thomas wrote while at Hare Hall Camp. Here he expresses his thoughts on the war and its destructive impact on all aspects of society. As Matthew Hollis comments,

> The poem he wrote may not have been a conventional war poem, but the war touched every part of it. It would be written into the storm and the fallen tree, into the missing man and in the mysterious lovers. It would bring together, as the war itself would, a confluence of class: labourer and poet, manual worker and man of leisure; archetypes and of course real men, who might meet again in France, where the furrow would become the trench.
> (*Now All Roads Lead to France*, page 285)

Some have suggested that the introduction of the lovers perhaps gives hope for life too.

  1 **the team's head brass**   the shining horse brasses on the harness of the ploughing team.
  6 **charlock**   a weed belonging to the mustard family, which has yellow flowers.
 10 **share**   ploughshare – the sharp blade that cuts through the soil.
20–21 **I could spare an arm... / A leg**   Note the detached and dispassionate tone here.
 26 **they killed him**   Again a detached tone is captured here.
 34 **for the last time**   This is an ambiguous phrase. What ideas or associations does it possess?

Bob's Lane

22 June 1916

This is another poem in which Thomas focuses on a solitary rural character, this time *Old Farmer Hayward of the Heath*. His love of life unites him with the natural world and he has become part of it. However, the poem ends on a darker note as his efforts to shape the natural world ultimately have a negative impact.

   3 **cob**   a stocky, thickset horse.
   7 **stormcock**   another name for the mistle (missel) thrush.
 15 **slough**   a muddy hollow.

Blenheim Oranges

3 September 1916

During the first part of September 1916, Thomas was stationed in Bloomsbury, London and was billeted at his parents' house in Balham. By this time he had been commissioned and was an officer cadet in the Royal Artillery. The poem begins with a gloomy, brooding tone and continues with a series of negative images as he reflects on both the past and the present.

 1–4 Note the repetition of *gone*. What effect does this have?
  11 **Blenheim oranges**   old type of English apple with a yellowish orange skin.
  12 **grubby**   What connotations does Thomas's use of the word hold here?
  14 **the lost one**   There is some doubt as to who this might be, although Edna Longley offers the possibility that it is a reference to Hope Webb.
17–24 Note the description of the house, now deserted and devoid of life. In the final two stanzas he goes on to compare it to himself.

Lights Out

November 1916

Thomas wrote this poem while at the Royal Artillery barracks at Trowbridge in Wiltshire, and it is one of several poems he wrote prompted by the bugle calls that punctuated the day in an army camp. In this instance the bugle call is 'lights out', which signals to the soldiers that they must turn out their lights and sleep. Thomas sent a draft of the poem to Eleanor Farjeon on 6 November and told her that the poem summed up what he had thought at hearing that call. Later she commented that she regarded it as 'his best-loved poem'. It 'goes into the unknown of himself further than any other' (Eleanor Farjeon, *Edward Thomas: The Last Four Years*, page 217).

> 3 **Forest** The image of a wood or forest is sometimes used by Thomas as a symbol of death.
> 7 Note the use of the image of the road (see headnote to *Roads*, page 98).

'Out in the dark over the snow'

24 December 1916

This poem was written at the cottage his wife Helen had moved into on 8 October in the village of High Beech in Essex, while Thomas was on his last leave before embarkation to France. Here again he contemplated the possibility of being killed in France. The overwhelming impression created by the poem is one of darkness and, as Andrew Motion comments, 'it stands as a conclusion to his own progress towards death' (*The Poetry of Edward Thomas*, page 134).

> 2–3 The young fallow deer (*fawns*) go with their mother (the *doe*).
>   6 The personification and language use here give the darkness a sinister edge.
>   9 **hound** This suggests a deer hound, used in deer hunting.
> 14 **Drums** Note the possible double meaning; the word has a military connotation.
> 15 **sage** wise.

Interpretations

It has often been said that the poetry of Edward Thomas is very difficult to categorize. He has been described as a 'nature poet' and a 'war poet'; he has been associated with the Georgian poets of the early twentieth century such as Walter de la Mare, Rupert Brooke and Lascelles Abercrombie, and with a completely opposing movement, the Imagists, typified by poets such as Ezra Pound, F.S. Flint and Richard Aldington.

Of course, Thomas knew all the poets in both camps and some of them were his friends. He had written critical reviews of the work of de la Mare, Pound and many more besides. As Cecil Day-Lewis (see Further Reading page 169) pointed out, Thomas 'was in the Georgian Movement but as a critic, rather than of it', and he never aligned himself with any particular movement.

Thomas was certainly interested in nature and the rural life and folk traditions of England, as were the Georgian poets. Their poetry, written before the First World War, has been characterized as overly sentimental, romanticized and escapist, as opposed to the realist First World War poets, and it was derided by Pound and the Imagists. Although both the Georgians and Thomas were opposed to the grandiose, rhetorical style of much of the poetry that had preceded them, the Georgians too often, in the words of Day-Lewis, 'produced a flat, trivial kind of poetry' that had no more merit than the overblown style they wished to replace. Day-Lewis goes on to point to a key difference between the poetry of the Georgians and Thomas's:

> What separates Edward Thomas from the ruck of his contemporaries is not so much his keen observation and familiar knowledge of nature as his attitude towards it – an attitude which expresses itself in a certain tone of voice and justifies itself by the hard core we feel in his poems.
> (Cecil Day-Lewis, 'The Poetry of Edward Thomas', page 75)

Although Thomas (like Imagists such as Ezra Pound) rejects the sentiment of some Victorian verse, and his poems exhibit some of the tenets the Imagists adhered to, he is no more an Imagist poet than a Georgian one.

It is also true that while many of Thomas's poems reveal the influence of being written against the background of a major war raging in Europe, they are not 'war poems' in the sense that we normally understand the label (see page 145). The truth is that there are elements of many ideas and influences in Thomas's poetry but for him, as F.R. Leavis (see page 161 and Further Reading) observed, the main concern is:

> with the finer texture of living, the here and now, the ordinary moments, in which for him the 'meaning' (if any) resides. It is as if he were trying to catch some shy intuition on the edge of consciousness which would disappear if looked at directly.
>
> (F.R. Leavis, *New Bearings in English Poetry*, page 55)

Themes and ideas

Just as Thomas cannot be neatly categorized as a poet, his poems cannot be neatly categorized on a strictly thematic basis. A single poem can explore a number of ideas, and often the apparent starting point of a poem is not the central idea he is exploring through it. However, there are certain ideas that are of central interest to Thomas and to which he returns repeatedly in his poetry.

Many of his poems explore ideas about the natural world, the rural landscape of England and a sense of the past. Other poems focus on the nature of memory, or feelings about himself, his melancholy or thoughts initiated by the war. All of his poems contain a number of ideas, suggestions or connotations that mesh together to create the effect upon the reader that Thomas sought. In the end, that effect might not provide answers or explanations, and a number of his poems end in what Michael Kirkham (see Further Reading) calls 'lucid uncertainty'. It is important, then, when reading the poems for yourself, that you remain alert to the various ways in which they can be viewed and interpreted, and bear in mind that sometimes there are not necessarily definitive explanations about their 'meaning'.

Landscape and the natural world

From an early age Thomas had shown a keen interest in nature and the natural world, and as a boy had loved his trips to rural Wiltshire or, at home, roaming in the urban wilderness of Wandsworth Common. As he grew up, he acquired an extensive knowledge of the flora and fauna of the countryside, of birdsong and wild flowers, and developed a sensitivity to the rhythms of the natural cycle. He recorded his observations in the extensive notebooks he kept. This fascination with the natural world and with the rural landscape of England is to be seen in much of his poetry.

When possible he walked, often covering 20 miles or more in a day, and he only cycled when he needed to cover longer distances. He believed that the speed of cycling did not allow him to observe the detail of the natural things around him. When he began to write poetry, it is no surprise that in many of his poems nature is such a key element. For these reasons, he is often regarded as a 'nature poet'. Certainly many of his poems focus closely on the natural world and the rural environment, but these poems are much more than simple 'nature poems' and do not simply describe the sights and sounds of nature around him. He uses specific details from the natural world to explore a range of complex ideas, such as the relationship between past and present, between humanity and the environment, or the English rural life and its characters and folk traditions. Thomas's view of nature and his relationship with it was complex and intense, and his need to experience it was a vital part of his being.

One of his earliest poems, *March*, illustrates this combination of an awareness of the natural world with complexity of thought. In the poem Thomas anticipates the coming of spring.

Activity

How does Thomas use nature to explore his ideas in *March*?

Discussion

The poem opens with Thomas seeing the sun appear on a cold day that follows a stormy day and night, expressing his certainty that spring will come again – *perhaps tomorrow* (32), but if it does not he has the patience to wait. The weather reminds him, too, that winter has not yet gone as he can feel *the cold burning / Of hail and wind* and see *the primroses / Torn by the hail* and *covered up in it* (4–6). The descriptions of the warmth of the sun, the melting hail, the sunset and the sense that spring was lost *in those mountains cold* (15) are effective in creating a sense of the natural scene and the anticipation often felt as we look for signs that spring is on its way.

In these opening 15 lines the focus has been on Thomas's responses to this false sense of spring, but at the heart of the poem are the thrushes, and the second part of the poem describes their responses. The opening question, *What did the thrushes know?*, immediately suggests that they are aware of something that Thomas is unaware of. They too had been quietened by the *Rain, snow, sleet, hail* (16), but in this brief interlude of sunshine at the end of the day, *They had but an hour to sing* (18). Note how Thomas stresses the eagerness of the thrushes to sing:

> On boughs they sang,
> On gates, on ground; they sang while they changed perches
> And while they fought, if they remembered to fight
>
> (lines 18–20)

They were not singing for joy, however; they were *unwilling* singers, but eager to:

> pack into that hour
> Their unwilling hoard of song before the moon
> Grew brighter than the clouds.
>
> (lines 21–23)

The silence of the night seems to hold a kind of threat that the thrushes want to ward off through their song. They sing to *keep off silence / And night* (24–25), and after night falls the silence is *Rich with all that riot of songs* but Thomas is unaware of this silence *till night had half its stars / And never a cloud* (29–31).

In another way, though, the silence offers a kind of promise of the return of spring, as Thomas becomes aware of the silence of night: *Rich with all that riot of songs, a silence / Saying that Spring returns, perhaps tomorrow* (30–31).

The poem leaves the reader, as so often in Thomas's poetry, with questions as to the relationship between the song and the silence. Judy Kendall (see Further Reading) sums up its importance as 'holding some undefined inexplicable knowledge that the listener, both while listening and for a short period afterwards, is enabled to share, if uncomprehendingly' (*Edward Thomas: The Origins of His Poetry*, pages 22–23).

In March, the song of the thrushes draws together the environment, the weather, the sense of silence and Thomas's presence in a moment of experience that is as profound as it is indefinable – a moment of the 'lucid uncertainty' described by Kirkham.

In '*But these things also*', Thomas lists the sights of nature that he sees as being emblematic of spring: *the roadside… grass / Long-dead*, the *shell of a little snail bleached*, a *chip of flint, and mite / Of chalk; and the small birds' dung* (2–7) – a list that, perhaps, surprises the reader.

Activity

Think about the title and the opening line of *'But these things also'*. What do you notice about the way these are phrased, and what ideas does Thomas go on to explore in the poem?

Discussion

The opening word *But* suggests the second part of a sentence, the first part being omitted. The suggestion is that this is the second part of a list, the first part of which contained the kinds of things that would normally come to mind as representing signs of spring. However, Thomas here focuses on the things that many would not notice or would be unaware of, and places these at the centre of the poem. These are the small, apparently insignificant details that Thomas observes and recognizes as also being part of spring's approach. Thomas's recognition that in the eyes of many people these small signs would go unnoticed is emphasized by opening with *But*.

Apart from being a rather surprising list, its emphasis is on whiteness: the snail's shell is *bleached*, the dung is in *splashes of purest white*, there is a *mite / Of chalk* (5–8). There is ambiguity here: white as a colour can be associated with lack of life, like the grass *that is greyer now / Than all the Winter it was* (3–4), whereas spring is a season of life and vibrancy. White is also the colour of purity, however, and it is paradoxical that it is here linked to dung. The very time of year that Thomas is describing, though, consists of elements of both winter and spring, as one season overlaps the other. Thomas uses this contrasting of opposites to reflect the nature of the season, as he does in *March*. The colours of spring have not yet arrived, although he knows its presence is close; he also knows that often things identifying the presence of spring are mistakenly identified, as in *All the white things a man mistakes / For earliest violets* (9–10), but as one season merges into the next, nature still has to *pay Winter's debts* (12).

In the final stanza the north wind continues to blow and the starlings that flock and chatter to *Keep their spirits up in the mist* (15) are reminiscent of the thrushes in *March*. But they sense the approach of spring, despite that fact that *Winter's not gone* (16). As Edna Longley comments: 'The interpenetration of English seasons is a recurrent focus and symbol in Thomas's writings . . . But while some poems harmonise different seasons, *But these things also* is left unresolved' (*The Annotated Collected Poems*, page 203).

This lack of resolution is apparent through the oppositions set up in the final line: *And Spring's here, Winter's not gone.*

In *The Hollow Wood* a bird, this time the *goldfinch*, is again a significant feature. In one sense Thomas presents here a picture of a decaying wood, but again there is a meaning contained in the poem that lies beneath the surface. The picture of the wood is disturbing, sinister, even nightmarish, making the contrast with the 'normality' of the goldfinch, outside the wood *in the sun*, even more marked.

Activity

Look at *The Hollow Wood* and make a list of the images that Thomas uses to create a negative impression of the wood.

Discussion

These are some points you may have noted.
- The use of the adjective *Hollow* in the title immediately creates a sense of a wood that is dead – the trees are hollow and decaying.
- In the hollow wood the birds *swim like fish* (4), creating an image of the unnatural which is further emphasized by the description of *Fish that laugh and shriek* (5), adding a nightmarish quality to the description.
- In line 7 the adjective *pale* is added to the description of the wood; the lack of colour builds up further the sense of a place with life drained out of it.
- *Lichen, ivy, and moss* (8) grow in the wood – these are often found growing on dead wood and in dank places, in a parasitic way. Ironically, though, it is this growth covering the trees that keeps them *evergreen* (9) and so gives the illusion of life.
- The description of the trees as standing *half-flayed and dying* and of *dead trees on their knees / In dog's-mercury, ivy, and moss* (10–12) personifies the trees and adds a sinister note of suffering. The reference to *dog's-mercury* further adds to this sense of unwholesomeness, as it is an extremely poisonous plant.

The 'goldfinch flits / Along the thistle-tops' (*The Hollow Wood*)

The *goldfinch* makes a marked contrast, being a brightly coloured bird with red and gold markings. It is *Out in the sun*, and its movements are full of life, as it *flits / Along the thistle-tops* feeding on the seeds, and gives the bright *twit* of its call (1–2). Unlike the unnatural and discordant sounds of the birds in the hollow wood, the goldfinch acts in a natural way. Thomas, then, has created two worlds for the reader to contemplate – one of gloom and decay, an unnatural and distorted world, and in contrast a natural world where life and brightness exist.

Some have suggested that the source of this poem lies in Thomas's melancholy and his sense of frustration. Cecil Day-Lewis comments: 'the *pale hollow wood* was his own heart, aware of itself dying by inches, and the *bright twit of the goldfinch*, dropping into it from outside'.

In a number of his poems, Thomas sets the transience of human existence against the background of the natural world. In *Swedes*, for example, he uses the commonplace agricultural procedure of storing root vegetables in order to bring into contrast the life of nature against the notion of the afterlife. The language Thomas uses to describe the sunlight falling on the uncovered swedes uses colours suggestive of the regal:

> They have let in the sun
> To the white and gold and purple of curled fronds
> Unsunned.

> (lines 2–4)

The *sight* of this is *more tender-gorgeous / At the wood-corner where Winter moans and drips* (4–5) than when a pharaoh's tomb was seen for the first time with *God and monkey, chariot and throne and vase, / Blue pottery, alabaster, and gold* (9–10).

Light is let in both to the swedes and to the pharaoh's tomb, but the swedes are the products of a living, natural world whereas what the light reveals in the tomb is beautiful but dead artefacts. For Thomas the difference lies in the fact that the *long-dead Amen-hotep* lies *dreamless* whereas Thomas experiences *a dream of Winter, sweet as Spring* (11–12), suggesting a renewal of life, through the seasonal re-birth brought by spring.

The two poems that Thomas included in his anthology *This England*, under the pseudonym Edward Eastaway – *The Manor Farm* and *Haymaking* – both capture the essence of the England that Thomas loved, and combine this with a sense of his own particular kind of patriotism. In *This England*, Thomas wanted to create an anthology of writing expressing the 'emotional meaning of England' and what is meant 'when a man speaks of England, especially since the war'. In putting the anthology together he had written to Eleanor Farjeon:

> I haven't made myself clear yet about the anthology. It isn't
> what Dickens 'says of England' that I want. Anything that
> makes us feel England particularly or which we could imagine
> making a stranger feel is what I want.
>
> (quoted by Eleanor Farjeon in *Edward Thomas:*
The Last Four Years, page 116)

As noted on page 94, his two poems were only included at the last minute when the publisher asked him to fill two blank pages that had arisen after typesetting. He clearly chose to include these two poems for what they say about England.

In *Haymaking* Thomas captures a sense of the harmony between humanity and nature through the traditional scene of haymaking. In the poem, Thomas portrays the labourers working in the fields in a way that had remained unchanged since before the time of *Clare and Cowper, Morland and Crome* (35).

Activity

Look at the opening section of *Haymaking* (lines 1–18) and examine how Thomas builds up an image of contentment through the rural scene.

Discussion

These are some of the points you may have noted.

- A sense of peace is established from the outset as day breaks – this is often a time of peace and tranquillity. The *night's thunder* has passed and the *fiery day* still possesses that early morning *kernel sweet of cold* (1–2). Note the effect of the metaphor here giving a sense of wholesomeness, suggestive in itself of the fruitfulness of harvest-time.
- Thomas uses contrasts: the dark of the night gives way to the dawn, and the warmth of the early morning sun still has a slight edge of cold.
- The simile of the first gods *swimming the stormless sea / In beauty and in divine gaiety* creates a sense of timelessness and

116

the peace that existed *before they made the world / And misery* (4–6).

- There is a linking of the seasons – *the holly's Autumn falls in June* (8) – similar to the running together of the seasons in *The Manor Farm*.
- The *smooth white empty road* (7) offers the possibility of both solitude and connectedness.
- The *mill-foot water tumbled white and lit / With tossing crystals* gives a feeling both of vitality and renewal, emphasized further by the simile *happier than any crowd / Of children pouring out of school aloud* (10–12).
- Even in the *thickets* the birds sing *unceasingly* and the swift shrieks *in his fierce glee* (13–17).

Thomas with his son Merfyn in 1900

From this opening scene portraying an active natural world in harmony, the poem moves into a series of images creating a sense of inactivity: the *Haymakers rested. The tosser lay forsook / Out in the sun,* the *long waggon stood / Without its team* which *seemed it never would / Move from the shadow of that single yew.* The *team* was *still,* the *labourers enjoyed the shade / That three squat oaks mid-field together made* (22–28). Thomas's references to the *yew* and the *oaks*, both types of tree capable of living hundreds of years, add to the timelessness of the scene, setting it in the context of all such scenes going back, unchanging, far into the past.

Activity

Look at the final part of *Haymaking* (lines 33–42). What is the significance of these closing lines?

Discussion

Thomas has frozen this scene – captured it as a moment in time that links directly back to the past, unchanged:

> All was old,
> This morning time, with great age untold,
> Older than Clare and Cowper, Morland and Crome,
> Than, at the field's far edge, the farmer's home,
> A white house crouched at the foot of a great tree.
>
> (lines 33–37)

Thomas's references to figures from the past associated with countryside, poets and painters of the English landscape and scenes of rural life, help to emphasize that link with the rural past. The scene is one that has been characteristic of England for centuries. At the end of the poem Thomas finds in the scene a kind of immortality, looking both backward into the past and forward into the future:

> Under the heavens that know not what years be
> The men, the beasts, the trees, the implements
> Uttered even what they will in times far hence –
> All of us gone out of the reach of change –
> Immortal in a picture of an old grange.
>
> (lines 38–42)

In *The Manor Farm* Thomas sees a similar vision of England. In the poem he creates a picture of the farm, the church and the yew-tree, *in age / Its equals and in size* (8–9), and together they *slept in a Sunday silentness* (10) – the sibilance here contributes to the effect of sleepy tranquillity. The scene is set within a natural context as the sun melts the ice of a February morning, with *the catkins wagging in the hedge* (3) and the only sound the swish of the horses' tails against *a solitary fly* (17). The scene presents a wholeness in which even the seasons become as one, and a sense of unchanging harmony is created:

> The Winter's cheek flushed as if he had drained
> Spring, Summer, and Autumn at a draught
> And smiled quietly. But 'twas not Winter –
> Rather a season of bliss unchangeable
> Awakened from farm and church where it had lain
> Safe under tile and thatch for ages since
> This England, Old already, was called Merry.
>
> (lines 18–24)

Note Thomas's use of capitalization for *Old* and *Merry* in these final lines, both of them linking to England – 'Old England' and 'Merry England' – and both creating a similar effect. 'Merry England' is a term often used for an idyllic, pastoral way of life in a time gone by. The *Manor Farm* is a kind of cultural symbol of this type of England. As in the closing lines of *Haymaking*, Thomas here captures quintessentially 'English' scenes from a kind of golden age of rural England, creating a picture of the England Thomas loves and that is central to his particular type of patriotism.

Character and narrative

When Thomas reviewed Robert Frost's *North of Boston* poetry collection, he pointed to one of the key qualities of Frost's verse, what Frost himself called 'the sound of sense'. This was Frost's term for the essential quality of the language of everyday life and the voice of authentic speech, which he used in his poetry rather than trying to create artificial poetic effects lacking in sincerity. This was very close to the view Thomas had long held about poetry. They both believed firmly that rhythm was the key element in a poem, and that the effect of rhythm was heard, rather than read on the page.

For both poets the rhythm of speech – what Frost called 'cadence' – rather than adhering to rigid poetic conventions of metre was vital in writing poetry that spoke to the reader. This 'cadence' is the natural rhythm and modulation of speech, and communicates meaning in much deeper terms than mere content, as it also conveys mood and atmosphere. Frost and Thomas had arrived by different routes at the very same view, and when Thomas wrote the following about the poems in *North of Boston* he was writing about poems that encapsulated his own views of poetry:

> These poems are revolutionary because they lack the exaggeration of rhetoric; and even at first sight appear to lack the poetic intensity of which rhetoric is an imitation. Their language is free from the poetical words and forms that are the chief material of secondary poets. The metre avoids not only the old-fashioned pomp and sweetness, but the later fashion also of discord and fuss. In fact, the medium is common speech.
>
> (*Daily News*, 22 July 1914)

In Thomas's first poem, *Up in the Wind*, which he based closely on a prose sketch he had written called *The White Horse*, he began to put his ideas into practice.

It has often been noted that these ideas are evident in the opening of the poem, which contains direct speech, using the rhythm and inflections of natural speech. The poem tells the story of a young countrywoman drawn back, at least partially unwillingly, to the place of her birth.

Activity

Look at the opening 11 lines of *Up in the Wind*. What do you notice about the ways in which Thomas conveys a convincing sense of natural speech here?

Discussion

Some key features that become immediately evident here include the following.

- The opening use of exclamations not only creates a dramatic opening but gives a sense of an authentic voice, showing the frustrations of the girl.
- The use of enjambment to allow the speech to flow naturally avoids creating artificial breaks and so helps create a sense of everyday speech.
- The use of a flexible metre breaking away from the strictly decasyllabic (10-syllable) form again allows Thomas to capture the variable rhythm pattern of natural speech.

Similar effects can be seen at various points in the poem, and they effectively reflect the tendency for speech to come in phrases. For example, look at lines such as:

> 'Did you ever see
> Our signboard?' No. The post and empty frame
> I knew.
>
> (lines 75–77)

and

> Now I should like to see a good white horse
> Swing there, a really beautiful white horse,
> Galloping one side, being painted on the other.
>
> (lines 81–83)

However, it has often been noted too that by the end of the poem other ideas that were of central importance to Thomas become evident. For example, see the closing lines:

> Between the open door
> And the trees two calves were wading in the pond,
> Grazing the water here and there and thinking,
> Sipping and thinking, both happily, neither long.
> The water wrinkled, but they sipped and thought,
> As careless of the wind as it of us.
> 'Look at those calves. Hark at the trees again.'
>
> (lines 109–115)

These lines reflect an important key idea that Thomas held. He believed it was important to use words that were in keeping with the character described, and which continued the rhythm pattern established in the direct speech, using blank verse but lengthening or shortening lines as required to convey the sense of 'the mixture of casual gossip and dramatic energy with which the poem spoke'. After the exclamatory, dramatic opening, very much in the style of Frost, Thomas makes the remainder of the poem very much his own. As Andrew Motion (see Further Reading) comments:

> the overtly dramatic was foreign to Thomas's nature, and he soon abandoned it in favour of a more reflective tone. The subdued and observant cadence, by departing from the stridency of the opening lines with their shower of exclamation marks, reflects in miniature Thomas's development as a poet.
>
> (*The Poetry of Edward Thomas*, page 70)

Up in the Wind allowed Thomas to begin to experiment with dialogue, and he developed this in different ways in poems such as *The Chalk Pit*. He started putting his ideas into practice, and over the next few months he returned, in different ways, to poems based around a central character. These often involve meeting solitary old men in lonely and isolated rural settings, in the same way as some of William Wordsworth's poems focus on individual characters who are so steeped in their rural landscape that they have almost become part of it. Thomas's poems on such themes include *The New Year, Man and Dog, May 23, Lob* and *Bob's Lane*. In some ways these poems present Thomas's response to the erosion of the traditional rural culture, which he explores through the various countrymen, tramps and gypsies he encounters.

In *The New Year*, Thomas meets an old man in the woods on the stormy morning of New Year's Day.

Activity

What kind of visual impression of the figure does Thomas create in *The New Year*, and what effects does he achieve?

Discussion

From a short distance away Thomas is unable to recognize the old man as a man at all:

> I could not tell how much
> Of the strange tripod was a man. His body,
> Bowed horizontal, was supported equally
> By legs at one end, by a rake at the other

> (lines 3–6)

This old man has been likened to the old leech gatherer in Wordsworth's poem *Resolution and Independence*. Note how the use of simile initially adds to the sense of confusion; he was *far less like a man than / His wheel-barrow in profile was like a pig* (7–8). A later simile emphasizes a sense of great age: *His head rolled under his cape like a tortoises's* (14).

There is little speech in this poem, but the one line there is, as far as the narrator can hear it through the roar of wind in the trees, is the response to him wishing the old man a Happy New Year – *Happy New*

Year, and may it come fastish, too (19). This suggests a whole range of unspoken meaning. Some have suggested that one of these unspoken meanings of the response is a reference to the war.

In *Man and Dog* and *May 23*, Thomas again centres his poems around solitary rural figures. *Man and Dog*, based closely on material from a notebook entry describing his meeting with an old man, is written in rhyming couplets, and reflects Thomas's awareness of the changing world and its impact on the old, itinerant labourer he meets. The old man, a representative of a dying breed of vagrant rural labourers, roams the countryside picking up casual labouring work where he can. Thomas gives us a brief but thorough history of the man's life, which reflects the social history of labourers like him towards the end of the nineteenth century, and at the beginning of the twentieth.

> His mind was running on the work he had done
> Since he left Christchurch in the New Forest, one
> Spring in the 'seventies, – navvying on dock and line
> From Southampton to Newcastle-on Tyne, –
> In 'seventy-four a year of soldiering
> With the Berkshires, – hoeing and harvesting
> In half the shires where corn and couch will grow.
>
> (lines 13–19)

Towards the end of the poem the old man shows a stoical acceptance of his position, knowing that he will find it difficult to find a makeshift bed at a farm, travelling, as he does, with his old dog. His feeling that, in the trenches, *Many a man sleeps worse tonight / Than I shall* (39–40) and his thoughts of the soldiers *marching after the enemy* (42) are a reminder of the looming presence of the war, even reaching into his nomadic rural life.

The final couplets of the poem and the final image of the man and his dog passing into the *twilight of the wood* have an elegiac feel to them, creating a sense that people like this old man and his way of life are rapidly disappearing:

> And there I nodded
> 'Good-night. You keep straight on.' Stiffly he plodded;
> And at his heels the crisp leaves scurried fast,
> And the leaf-coloured robin watched. They passed,
> The robin till next day, the man for good.
> Together in the twilight of the wood.

> (lines 43–48)

Kirkham comments that 'The life of nature is manifested and valued by Thomas in animals and in the general folk life. The latter makes its appearance in poems which salute the musical and poetic folk traditions' (*The Imagination of Edward Thomas*, page 94). In *The Gypsy*, Thomas presents another group of people who live on the fringes of society. Although they are not solitary figures they play a similar role to the lone men in some of the poems mentioned above. In one sense they are outside the mainstream of society, and like Thomas's solitary figures they are also an integral part of rural landscapes and traditions. The way they are pushed to the margins of society is symbolized by the fact that they have no fixed point, no land to call their own, and they make their homes on commons and wasteland. Their nomadic lifestyle, however, has a permanence that seems immune to the changes in the society around them, and represents a certain kind of wildness; they live according to their own laws, but contain a vitality of their own. This vitality is seen not just through the *rascally Bacchanal dance* (17) but also in the spark of the gypsy boy's black eyes, in comparison to which the poet seems *Like a ghost new-arrived* (25).

Gypsy families with their caravans in the 1910s; their nomadic way of
life made them part of rural landscapes and traditions

May 23 presents another solitary figure, that of *Old Jack
Noman* (12).

The poem begins by creating a sense of the beauty of the
day, but immediately this is overshadowed by a note of regret
that past days were not perfect, and foreboding that the weather
cannot last for the following days:

> But though fair and clear the two behind
> Seemed pursued by tempests overpast;
> And the morrow with fear that it could not last
> Was spoiled.
>
> (lines 4–7)

Sure enough, *ere the stones were warm* (7) a storm had broken.
At midday *Old Jack Noman appeared again* (12), giving the sense

that he appears from time to time as he leads his nomadic, itinerant lifestyle.

Activity

What significance do you see in the name *Jack Noman*?

Discussion

Unlike the character in *Man and Dog*, who is unnamed, the character here is given an identity through his name and the fact that the narrator has met him before. However, there may be more significance in the name too. It has been pointed out that Jack is a name traditionally given to English folk heroes, such as Jack in the Green, a figure in traditional May Day celebrations, and that the name also crops up in many folk tales such as 'Jack and the Beanstalk'.

The name *Noman* also holds significance here. For Thomas, figures such as this encapsulated the spirit of rural England and so the character represents 'no man' and therefore 'every man' in a symbolic sense. The term 'No Man' also carries connotations of 'No Man's Land', literally meaning land belonging to no one, in reference to the fact that the character has no ties and spends much of his life in wild and open country. It also, of course, holds connotations of the no-man's land of the trench warfare on the Western Front.

Activity

Compare Thomas's presentation of *Old Jack Noman* with his presentation of the old man in *Man and Dog* and the characters in *The Gypsy*. Explore any similarities you find between the poems.

Discussion

You may have thought of the following points.
* Like the old man in *Man and Dog*, who is *lame* (6), Jack Noman is old and *crooked*, but Noman is also *tall* (13).

- He has a bunch of cowslips in his *button-hole* and more in his *cap* (15–16). This suggests his link to the natural world.
- The connection with nature is further emphasized through the similes: *He was welcome as the nightingale* (18), and he was tanned the colour of the *leaf and bur / That clung to his coat* (22–23) – his tanned skin makes him the colour of the earth itself.
- The link with nature is further emphasized as he appears on *the first day that the midges bit* (39), as if he is a harbinger of summer.
- Noman, like the gypsies, lives according to his own law; the fact that he lives off the land is seen in the suggestion that his watercress has come from a dubious source and so Thomas cannot buy it. Like the gypsies too, he shows a generosity of spirit when he gives the cress away, together with his flowers.
- He 'disappears' at the end of the poem. In one sense this could be read as meaning that he simply moves on somewhere else, but Thomas's phrasing of the final lines of the poems suggests a symbolic meaning: *May the twenty-third, / The day Jack Noman disappeared*. The final stress being on *disappeared* raises the possibility of there being a more universal significance here, perhaps referring to the disappearance of the rural way of life and the world that characters such as Jack inhabited.

Lob is the culmination of Thomas's exploration of the lives of these rural, solitary figures, whom he regarded as being representative of a rural scene he knew was rapidly disappearing. Like *Jack Noman*, the name *Lob* also has its roots deep in English folklore, and like him and the unnamed man in *Man and Dog*, Lob is a solitary, itinerant rural figure. Longley sees him as 'a mythological figure able to sum up the English character and the character of England as they have evolved through time, in landscape, and in language' (*Poems and Last Poems*, page 268). Lob's close association with the soil is established early in the poem.

Activity

Look at the opening section of *Lob* (lines 1–12). How does Thomas create a link between Lob and his landscape here? What other effects does this section create?

Discussion

Time itself is measured by the natural world here; the opening words *At hawthorn-time* describe the time of year. The old man's face is described as being *weather cut / And coloured* (3–4) by the elements, just as a rock or part of the landscape might be shaped and worn by the weather. The colour of his face is also described using a simile drawn from the natural world: it is *rough, brown, sweet as any nut*. It is a *land face, sea-blue-eyed* (4–5). A sense of history is also established here, both in terms of Lob's own – it was 60 years since they had excavated the barrows, *while I was scaring sparrows* (10) – but also in a broader context. The barrows (burial mounds from ancient times) are an important feature of the landscape.

The narrator is actively seeking Lob, a figure from his past, from his memories. His search is complicated because of the numerous villages and because *My memory could not decide* (16) on the right place. Thomas's interest in names is clear as he illustrates the repetition and complication of local place names, in lines 14–17. This playing with names is similar to the contemplation on place names in his poem *Words*, which emphasizes the importance of names to a sense of place. Here the names also give a sense of the rural history of the place.

The *squire's son* (43) is able to give Thomas more information, and his description changes the focus and direction of the poem.

Activity

Look at the direction the poem takes in lines 43–78. What aspects does Thomas seem interested in exploring here?

Discussion

The poem, and Lob as a character, take on a more symbolic significance in these lines, and as Andrew Motion puts it, 'the pursuit of the individual is exchanged for the pursuit of what he represents' (*The Poetry of Edward Thomas*, page 105). The focus now becomes Lob's 'Englishness' and all that that entails – *He is English as this gate* (55), *He has been in England as long as dove and daw* (58), he gave the flowers of England their folk names, and other geographical features their colloquial names, and *Our blackbirds sang no English* (67) before he was there to hear and respond to them. Lob has ceased to be regarded as an individual, and has become a symbol of 'Englishness' representing the spirit and essence of the country.

The final part of the poem introduces a sense of threat and menace as, for the first time, there is direct reference to the war. Motion detects that this first appears as the poem changes Lob's name to Hob (101):

> By changing his hero's name to 'Hob' Thomas recalls 'old shepherd Hobbe, Crimea veteran' from the essay 'It's a long long way' (itself an account of the war's effect on English people in the provinces).
>
> (*The Poetry of Edward Thomas*, page 107)

Activity

Look at the final 50 lines of the poem and make a list of the references that might suggest a threat such as that brought by the war.

Discussion

You may have found the following examples.
- The reference to the *giant coming to destroy / Shrewsbury by flood* (114–115) introduces a note of menace.
- The lines *He, too, ground up the miller, / The Yorkshireman who ground men's bones for flour* (128–129) have clear connotations

of violence (note that the reference to grinding bones is repeated in line 142).

•   The reference to No Man's Land associates Lob with the war, but also all English battles of the past are represented by the selection of names of iconic English battles that determined the course of the country's future:

One of the lords of No Man's Land, good Lob, –
Although he was seen dying at Waterloo,
Hastings, Agincourt, and Sedgemoor, too, –
Lives yet.

(lines 138–141)

The significance of these references to battles is open to some interpretation, and there are varying views. Longley sees these references as indicating 'the uncrushable spirit of the common soldier still fighting to defend his country' (*Poems and Last Poems*, page 252). Others, though, see Thomas as being more cautious than this, believing that the spirit of England depends on the survival of the local identities, folk memories and characteristics that give it its special nature.

Lob, like *May 23*, ends on an ominous note; the speaker *disappeared* (145), as Jack Noman had done. The final description creates an image of him almost being absorbed *In hazel and thorn tangled with old-man's-beard* (146).

Motion sums up the poem like this:

throughout the conclusion Thomas is poised between celebration and anxiety. At the same time as he provides a beautifully complete account of his patriotic motives, he also admits that he is fighting for a territory with a 'culture and way of life which, ironically, he knew was disappearing'. The war, he realised, would be the final blow whether it was won or lost, but such certitude did not prevent him from rejoicing in those elements of the ancient culture which remained.

(*The Poetry of Edward Thomas*, page 110)

Memory and the past

In many of Thomas's poems memory, or memories of the past, play a central part and he writes about these ideas in many different ways. Sometimes he may explore thoughts of an England of the past such as in *The Manor Farm* or *The Combe*; sometimes a moment in time is captured as a memory such as in *Adlestrop*. In other poems it may be that an indistinct memory is triggered by something such as the smell of the herb in *Old Man*, or the parsley flower in *It Rains*, or the song of a bird as in *The Unknown Bird*; or perhaps an event provokes thoughts of the past and the memories it contains, such as in *Parting*.

In *Old Man*, one of Thomas's best-known poems, and only the fourth one he wrote, he explores the connection between the scent of the herb named in the title and the memories it evokes.

Activity

Look at the first stanza of *Old Man*. What paradoxes are created in these opening lines?

Discussion

In this opening stanza Thomas considers the names of the herb, *Old Man, or Lad's-love*, and the gap between these names and the plant itself. The names seem to have no connection with the plant or describe in any way the thing they name. Someone who does not know the plant would learn nothing about it from these names. Although on one level the names are interesting and colourful, they are also confusing and puzzling: *Even to one that knows it well, the names / Half decorate, half perplex, the thing it is* (lines 5-6).

The alternative names for the plant also appear contradictory and so obscure their meaning still further, as they contain the opposite ideas of age and youth. The herb grows with *rosemary*, traditionally symbolizing remembrance, and *lavender*, which has connotations of love, protection, purification and longevity. Despite the apparent contradictions of the names, however, Thomas likes them. But the real essence of the plant for him is that part of the herb that remains with him *In spite of time* (8).

Thomas goes on to develop ideas about his feeling for the herb, continuing the sense of contradiction established in the first stanza: *The herb itself I like not, but for certain / I love it* (lines 9–10).

The introduction of the idea of memories, though, begins to reconcile this apparent paradox, in that he loves it:

as some day the child will love it
Who plucks a feather from the door-side bush
Whenever she goes in or out of the house.

(lines 10–12)

He goes on to explain how the scent of this herb remains on her fingers. Notice here how Thomas creates a link between the child and the bush: *The bush is still / But half as tall as she, though it is as old* (lines 16–17).

Thinking of the child, the narrator can only wonder how much she will remember later, as she grows, of the specific times she plucked the leaves and smelled the scent on her fingers – how far her memory will recall the garden, the path, the cottage door, and the narrator himself telling her not to pick it.

Activity

Now look at the final two stanzas of *Old Man*. What ideas does Thomas develop here, and how does he achieve his effects?

Discussion

The poem's focus here shifts back on to the narrator himself as he knows he has lost the memories associated with the time that he first *met the bitter scent* (25), and all his attempts to retrieve these memories are in vain:

I, too, often shrivel the grey shreds,
Sniff them and think and sniff again and try
Once more to think what it is I am remembering,
Always in vain.

(lines 26–29)

His use of the present tense as he tries to think *what it is I am remembering* suggests that somewhere in his mind he is conscious of a memory, but his frustration comes from its elusiveness. His awareness of this and the fact that he has not given up hope of re-capturing the memory leads him to feel that, although *I cannot like the scent, / Yet I would rather give up others more sweet, / With no meaning, than this bitter one* (29–31).

In the final stanza, the tone of the poem is less optimistic. The memory cannot be unlocked because *I have mislaid the key* (32). The scent cannot be linked with a memory, although he tries again and again, sniffing the rubbed leaves of the herb; all his attempts end in failure. The past is lost to him, and so is the memory of any happiness he once experienced there. The idea of retrieving the memory is so important to him that he is not simply seeking it, he is *listening, lying in wait / For what I should, yet never can, remember* (34–35). The negativity of this experience is emphasized through the language here; the repetition of *nothing* and *no*, the use of *never* and the listing of what does not appear to him – *Neither father nor mother, nor any playmate* (38) – all increase the sense of isolation. The only thing that appears to him is an avenue, but it is one that the last words of the poem describe as *dark, nameless, without end*.

In *The Unknown Bird* Thomas attempts to recapture an intense experience of four or five years before, but it is blurred by memory and cannot be fully recalled. The poem opens with the narrator recalling the song of the bird he had heard several years before:

Three lovely notes he whistled, too soft to be heard
If others sang; but others never sang
In the great beech-wood all that May and June.

No one saw him: I alone could hear him
Though many listened. Was it but four years
Ago? or five? He never came again.

(lines 1–6)

Activity

Think about the opening lines of *The Unknown Bird*, above. What do you detect in them to suggest that the experience of hearing this birdsong was a mysterious and ethereal one?

Discussion

You may have thought of the following points.

- The notes of the birdsong are elusive and *too soft to be heard* while other birds sang.
- No other birds sang in the wood *all that May and June*.
- *No one* ever saw the bird.
- Only the narrator could hear the bird, although *many listened* for it.
- After the time he is remembering, the bird *never came again*.
- The questioning of when this took place – *four years / Ago? or five?* – suggests the intangible nature of the experience, difficult to place even in time.

As the poem develops, further indications of mystery appear. Often when the narrator heard the bird he was alone, and the bird usually seemed far off: *As if a cock crowed past the edge of the world, / As if the bird or I were in a dream* (10–11). The bird sometimes appeared to be close to the narrator and yet, paradoxically, far away too. Naturalists could not identify the bird, but the notes that the narrator heard haunt him still. The feelings that the notes provoked in him create another paradox, in that he felt both joy and sadness on hearing the song:

Sad more than joyful it was, if I must say
That it was one or other, but if sad

135

'Twas sad only with joy too, too far off
For me to taste it.

(lines 22–25)

As in *Old Man*, memory is elusive; although he remembers the song and the way it made him feel, the memory is unreliable in other ways. He admits that he cannot *truly* tell if all the days when he heard the unknown bird were *fair* (26), but it seems to him now that they were. He does know, though, that whether he is happy or *suffering / A heavy body and a heavy heart* (29–30), whenever he thinks of that bird he finds comfort and a temporary escape from his trouble; he becomes *Light as that bird wandering beyond my shore* (32.)

Motion feels that the poem illustrates 'Thomas's hard-won certainty that fulfilment could only be achieved by reconciling "sadness" and "joy"' (*The Poetry of Edward Thomas*, page 158).

In *Adlestrop*, Thomas tries to capture another moment of intense feeling, and just as in *Old Man* a name has an important part to play in unfolding the ideas of the poem. It records an unscheduled stop made by Thomas's train at the small country station of Adlestrop in Gloucestershire.

Activity

How does Thomas use an outwardly small event to present and develop his ideas in *Adlestrop*?

Discussion

The name *Adlestrop* is the key that triggers the memory in the poem – a memory that Thomas begins to develop in a prosaic conversational tone, consisting of short, simple sentences that succinctly sum up the key elements of the scene:

It was late June.

The steam hissed. Someone cleared his throat.

> No one left and no one came
> On the bare platform. What I saw
> Was Adlestrop – only the name

(lines 4–8)

Kirkham notes that the 'bare disjointed notation of this event, and the fragmentary rhythms' contribute to the overall effect – that nothing happens (*The Imagination of Edward Thomas*, page 115).

In the third stanza, however, Thomas's attention shifts to the natural scene, with a list of the names of wild flowers glimpsed in that moment from the train, capturing the peace and tranquillity of the scene. The sense of stillness is further emphasized by a comparison with the clouds in the sky:

> And willows, willow-herb, and grass,
> And meadowsweet, and haycocks dry,
> No whit less still and lonely fair
> Than the high cloudlets in the sky.

(lines 9–12)

The repetition of *And* here builds and opens out the scene, then attention switches to *the sky*, increasing the feeling of space and capturing a sense of harmony.

In the final stanza the emphasis is on sound rather than sight, as the song of a blackbird captures the narrator's attention. He can hear a single blackbird, but symbolically it represents the universality of nature, the sound of the single bird becoming *mistier* and merging with, *Farther and farther, all the birds / Of Oxfordshire and Gloucestershire* (14–16).

Notice how, as Thomas moves from the 'real' world of the train, the platform, and someone clearing his throat, to the natural world and out into an ever-widening countryside, he has frozen a moment, like the moment in *Haymaking*, and imbued it with a kind of immortality locked in memory.

In *Parting*, Thomas explores ideas about the past and memory in a very different way. The poem is generally thought to have

Adlestrop railway station in the early years of the twentieth century, with an express train approaching

been inspired by Thomas's parting from his son, Merfyn, who was leaving with Robert Frost and his family to visit America for a while. Thomas had not enjoyed a close relationship with his son, and in the poem he reflects on how the past cannot be affected or changed by the present:

> The Past is a strange land, most strange.
> Wind blows not there, nor does rain fall:
> If they do, they cannot hurt at all.

> (lines 1–3)

Memories of both joy and misery in the past bring with them joy or sadness, so, for the narrator, *memory made / Parting today a double pain* (12–13). The first pain is because of the very act of parting itself, and the second is *Because the ill it ended vexed / And mocked me from the Past again* (15–16).

He feels that although the parting has ended an immediate unhappiness, nothing can change what has gone before; that unhappiness is forever locked in the past and nothing can change it or make amends for it. This poem presents a very personal vision of interlocking memories of the past.

In other poems such as *The Manor Farm* and *The Combe*, Thomas evokes a sense of the past of England through its landscape and nature, presenting a particular view of and feeling for the country and all it represented to him.

In *Celandine*, Thomas explores memory and the way it can distort the truth to create a new 'reality'. In the first stanza he thinks about a girl he knew, and this saddens him until he sees the sun on the celandines and the sight of these brings her to his mind in a different way: *she stood up like a flame, / A living thing* (3–4), re-created through the power of memory as if she was real again, and not:

> The shadow I was growing to love almost,
> The phantom, not the creature with bright eye
> That I had thought never to see, once lost.

(lines 5–7)

Activity

How does Thomas develop this idea further in stanza 2 of *Celandine*, and how do the final five lines of the poem reveal the 'truth'?

Discussion

In the second stanza he develops the picture of the girl in his mind, a memory linked to the initial sight of the celandines. Like the celandine that flowers for a short time, and is often called the 'spring messenger' because of its early flowering, in his memory the girl *wore / Her brightest bloom among the winter hues* (12–13). She appears fleetingly to him in his imagination, as she *laughed, with locks sweeping the mossy sod* (18).

In the final stanza, however, he faces the truth that what he has seen is not real, it was *a dream* (19), a kind of fantasy created through his imagination. This realization is triggered when he plucks a petal from the flower and smells its juice, which *made me sigh, remembering she was no more* (22). Like the smell of the herb in *Old Man*, the scene brings the realization that his memory of her is *Gone like a never perfectly recalled air* (23).

The 'other self'

In his prose work *In Pursuit of Spring*, Thomas wrote about a figure he referred to as the 'Other Man' who seemed to follow him, and accompanied him at various points on his journey. Longley refers to the 'Other Man' as 'Thomas's most sustained prose self-portrait and self-parody, exaggerating his literary predilections and problems, his love of nature and traditional things, his melancholy introversion' (*Poems and Last Poems*, page 165).

In his poem *The Other*, a similar figure appears who seems to be the narrator's double, but here the situation is reversed and it is the narrator who pursues him. Thomas's depressions and bouts of 'melancholy' are well documented. In 1911 he had written to a friend hoping that vegetarianism 'will cure my head, which is almost always wrong now – a sort of conspiracy going on in it which leaves me only a joint tenancy and a perpetual scare of the other tenant and wonder what he will do' (quoted by Longley in *Poems and Last Poems*, page 163).

Various critics have commented on the poem as one that represents the conflicts of Thomas's inner life, his insecurities, his uneasiness with the social world, and his sense of isolation. It also depicts his search for self-knowledge through the sustained use of two key symbols in his poetry, forests and roads.

Activity

Look at the opening stanza of *The Other*. What effect does Thomas create here?

Discussion

The short, abrupt opening sentence captures the sense of release the narrator feels as the *forest* comes to an end. The forest is often used by Thomas as a symbol of darkness and alienation, and the narrator is glad to escape it and return to the world. The depiction of the senses here emphasizes the change from the forest to *what's not forest* (7). Note how he can *feel* the light (2) – in the second stanza he can *taste* the sunlight (15). The unusual use of verbs here gives a striking sense of the tangibility of the light, emphasizing its importance in contrast to the darkness of the forest. He can *hear the hum / Of bees, and smell the drying grass / And the sweet mint* (2–4).

Emerging from the wood, he finds *both road and inn* (6), the inn offering the social world and the possibility of communication with others. At the inn, though, he is mistaken for another man who passed that way the day before and spent the night at the inn. He feels *fear* (10).

So begins the narrator's quest to catch up with his double. Day after day he pursues him, but *The Other* is always one step ahead. In the process of searching for him, however, the narrator does find out things about him. He finds from people he meets that although *like me in general* he is different in one important respect: *He had pleased them, but I less* (50–51). His double possesses the ability to relate to others in a social context. The narrator continues on *in solitude* (61). Human society seems indifferent to him, and his despair deepens to the point where he contemplates suicide, but rejects it:

Many and many a day like this
Aimed at the unseen moving goal

> And nothing found but remedies
> For all desire.[...]
>   And yet
> Life stayed on within my soul.
>
> (lines 31–38)

At the end of the poem the narrator is confronted by his double but cannot respond; instead he *slipped away* (100). He knows, however, that he must continue to pursue his double, even if his pursuit has changed:

> And now I dare not follow after
> Too close. I try to keep in sight,
> Dreading his frown and worse his laughter.
>
> (lines 101–103)

He recognizes now the unbreakable link between himself and his double; he cannot do any other than follow as his double is another aspect of his own personality, he is the 'other tenant' Thomas described as being in his head – *He goes: I follow: no release / Until he ceases. Then I also shall cease* (109–110).

In Kirkham's view, Thomas is now

> without illusions: he recognises equally the inescapable
> compulsion to search for social gratification and the
> impossibility of success... The core of self-knowledge
> and self-acceptance has been reached in the recognition that
> his scope is limited to what can be accomplished
> by withdrawal from, rather than co-operation with,
> society.
>
> (*The Imagination of Edward Thomas*, pages 63–64)

In several of his poems Thomas reflects on his own state of mind and his melancholy. In *Aspens*, for example, where he identifies himself with the aspen trees, his melancholy must be endured as a part of his 'self'. He also focuses on his melancholy in *Beauty* and *Melancholy*.

Activity

Compare the ways in which Thomas explores his ideas in *Beauty* and *Melancholy*.

Discussion

In *Beauty* the narrator begins by questioning his own feelings, aware that there is nothing that can please him now. He is contemptuous of his own self-pitying emotions:

> And yet I almost dare to laugh
> Because I sit and frame an epitaph –
> 'Here lies all that no one loved of him
> And that loved no one.'

(lines 3–6)

That *whim* passes in an instant, though, as he articulates his feelings more closely through a simile; he says he is *like a river / At fall of evening* (7–8) that is never warmed or lit by the sun, while the image of *Cross breezes* cutting *the surface to a file* (10) creates a harsh effect. Even though he feels like this, however, *some fraction of* him appreciates the scenes of nature that he visualizes: *There I find my rest, as through the dusk air / Flies what yet lives in me: Beauty is there* (17–18).

'Melancholy' was one of the terms Thomas used to describe his own feelings of unhappiness, and his poem of that name opens by describing the *rain and wind*. The repetition and the use of alliteration in the opening line give an impression of the driving nature of the *Summer storm*. At the heart of the narrator's condition is the contradiction it presents:

> so that if I feared the solitude
> Far more I feared all company: too sharp, too rude,
> Had been the wisest or the dearest human voice.
> What I desired I knew not, but whate'er my choice
> Vain it must be, I knew.

(lines 3–7)

It is the recognition of the contradictory elements of his *melancholy* that gives him some control over it:

> Yet naught did my despair
> But sweeten the strange sweetness, while through the wild air
> All day long I heard a distant cuckoo calling
> And, soft as dulcimers, sounds of near water falling
>
> (lines 7–10)

Thomas was only too aware of the fact that life brought hardships and frustrations, and in *The Glory* he explores his own feelings of disappointment and lack of fulfilment, even at times when he should feel happiness and joy.

Activity

Look at the opening of *The Glory* (lines 1–12). What paradox does Thomas present here?

Discussion

The title of the poem reflects the glory of the beautiful scene that presents itself to him one morning. Everything seems perfect: the dew is *untouched* (2), the sky has clouds *fair as new-mown hay* (5), and the birds are singing; the whole scene is fresh, and all seems possible. The dove *tempts me on to something sweeter than love* (4), urging him to seek perfection. However, instead of bringing him joy and comfort, the scene leaves him *scorning / All I can ever do, all I can be* (8–9). His own feelings of inadequacy, of failing to fulfil his potential and achieve his goals in life, make him feel he is not even fit to *dwell / In beauty's presence* (11–12) as he faces his own failings.

This thought causes him to think about what he should do next and he is faced with a dilemma.

Activity

What questions does Thomas pose to himself in the remainder of the poem? Does he find an answer?

Discussion

He questions whether he should try to respond to this beauty by *Hearkening to short-lived happy-seeming things* (17) in order to find what he seeks, or whether he should accept his limitations and frustrations and *be content with discontent* (19). One of his dilemmas is understanding what he means himself by *happiness*, and how he will be able to decide whether he has achieved it. This causes him to question whether he should give up altogether, to *let all go, / Glad, weary, or both* (23–24). He wonders if, perhaps, he has often been happy in the past and has not realized it, has not recognized happiness for what it is, or has been happy and has forgotten it in the withdrawn state he is trapped in – *fast pent* (26).

The ending of the poem is ambiguous and some have seen in the closing lines hints that Thomas sees a potential escape from the *dreary-swift* passage of time. Others see the ending more bleakly, in that he recognizes that he can never find fulfilment, and *cannot bite the day to the core*.

Thomas as a war poet

The question of whether Thomas is a 'war poet' is one that has sparked critical debate over many years. Some have pointed to the fact that only one of his poems, *'This is no case of petty right or wrong'*, is overtly about the war, while others refer to the many more subtle references or nuances suggestive of the war that are to be found in his poems.

Perhaps the issue is made less clear because of the nature of the poets we have become used to regarding as 'war poets'. In poetry such as that of Wilfred Owen, Siegfried Sassoon and Isaac Rosenberg there is no mistaking the fact that the dominant subject is clearly the war and that many of the poems are based closely on the poets' experiences of the fighting. The 'war poems' we are familiar with focus very much on scenes of battle, portraying the horror of the conditions men had to endure on the Western

Front, and the suffering and death of soldiers in the trenches. Thomas's poetry contains none of these things, but nevertheless many of his poems are at least in part concerned with the war. All of Thomas's poems were written during wartime; he clearly gave much thought to his own response to the war, and so it would be no surprise if the war exerted influence on his work.

His focus is, however, very different from that of most other 'war poets'; his concerns are not the same as those shown in poetry that is more overtly related to the war. As Motion puts it, 'Often... a single reference to the war provides an urgency which ripples through the entire poem' (*The Poetry of Edward Thomas*, page 119).

Tears was written in January 1915, just a few months before Thomas enlisted in the army and at a time when he was giving a great deal of thought to the direction his future should take. The time was rapidly approaching when he would need to choose between going with Frost to America or enlisting in the army and going to war. A few months later, his decision made, he enlisted in the Artists' Rifles (see page 14).

Activity

What view of England do you think Thomas presents in *Tears*? Do you detect any ambiguity in it?

Discussion

Thomas presents two traditional images of England here, the fox-hunting scene and the changing of the guard at the Tower of London. Both of these seem to present archetypical images of England, and perhaps hint at a patriotic tone, but there are ambiguities here. The title of the poem itself presents an ambiguity, in that tears can be shed through joy or sadness.

In the opening line the narrator tells us that he had *no tears left*, perhaps suggesting they had all been shed, and he was experiencing a kind of emotional exhaustion. They were shed the day *twenty hounds streamed by me, not yet combed out* (3). This presents an image of young soldiers who have been moulded together into a destructive force acting as one, *in their rage of gladness* (4). Note the simile in the following line: they were *made one, like a great dragon* as they tore across *Blooming Meadow*. This was the name given to the meadow at Elses Farm where the Thomas family had once lived and had been happy; it is symbolic of the rural England Thomas loves. It is a meadow, though, that *once bore hops* – but no more (7).

The second image that Thomas presents us with here is of the changing of the guard at the *double-shadowed Tower* (8). He presents the soldiers as young men drawn from the countryside of England and, like the soldiers fighting in France, country lads *Fair-haired and ruddy* who are being turned into disciplined fighters. They are given all the trappings of a martial scene with the *Drums* and *fifes* playing a patriotic, stirring tune that in itself harks back to a time before Waterloo, *The British Grenadiers* (14–15). The narrator's sense of *solitude / And silence* is pierced by the music, and this sight and sound give a fleeting insight which *told me truths I had not dreamed, / And have forgotten since their beauty passed* (16–18),

Kirkham says of this poem: 'there seem to be two *images* of England, one superimposed upon the other, which are felt to be incompatible'. He feels that the poet's tears are for '*rural* England, the England that was most dear to Thomas' which 'is menaced... by the dragon of war'. These two images have become united, but 'there are actually more than these two aspects of England in the poem: we have a military and a civil, a past and a present, perhaps a patrician and a plebeian England' (*The Imagination of Edward Thomas*, page 124).

In *The Owl*, written the following month, again Thomas draws a connection between military and civilian life. This time he begins by drawing attention to his own needs, and the experience of finding food and rest at the inn. The call of the owl outside causes him to think about all who could not find the shelter and sustenance he enjoyed, of the *Soldiers and poor, unable to rejoice* (16).

Thomas's most overt poem about the war is '*This is no case of petty right or wrong*', and in it he makes his view completely clear.

147

Activity

In *'This is no case of petty right or wrong'* Thomas addresses a particular aspect of the war that he feels strongly about. Summarize the views that he reveals here.

Discussion

The poem was written on 26 December 1915, when Thomas had been in the army for six months. It is well documented that Thomas had a deep loathing of the jingoistic attitude towards the war whipped up by the press and others. Thomas's own father held these attitudes and Thomas had argued with him about the war that Christmas. Perhaps the first thing to note about the poem is the angry tone that Thomas captures as he presents what Motion calls his 'reasoned rejection of tub-thumping'.

- He opens by clearly stating that the war is too complex to be reduced to the simple black and white, right and wrong terms that some would have us believe in.
- He refuses to allow newspapers to whip him up into a patriotic frenzy that distorts judgement. The use of the term *fat* to describe the *patriot* here (5) suggests an element of complacency on the part of those who sit back and shout about patriotic fervour while themselves doing little for their country.
- He recognizes that it is not a simple choice between *the Kaiser* and the *fat patriot*, but the issues have become obscured by the din of *war and argument* which is no more meaningful than the *storm smoking along the wind / Athwart the wood* (10–12). Note the imagery of threat and danger here in *storm* and *smoking*, together with sense of evil – *Two witches' cauldrons* – in the following line. Note too, the sense of the clamour of the battlefield in the words *Dinned* (9) and *roar* (12); the imagery here is reminiscent of Shakespeare's *Macbeth*.
- Out of the chaos, a new England will be born, but not a 'different' England. Unlike many of this contemporaries Thomas did not want a new, changed England but one in the image of the old, one *like her mother that died yesterday* (15), like the *phoenix* rising from the *ashes* (18–19).

- He is not interested in the conclusions that future historians might come to in their analysis of the war and its causes. His interest is in England – the England that he loves – and its defence. In that sense, the enemy of England is his enemy too:

> She is all we know and live by, and we trust
> She is good and must endure, loving her so:
> And as we love ourselves we hate her foe.

(lines 24–26)

Others among Thomas's poems that reveal ideas connected to the war are much less direct in the expression of views. For example, *The Mill-Pond*, written a few months before his enlistment, contains no overt references to the war, but some have suggested that the girl's warning to *Take care!* and the bursting storm that shatters the peace and tranquillity of the day, causing the narrator to take shelter, hint at the presence of war. In *February Afternoon*, although the starting point is the natural world, the presence of war is closer to the surface. In the first line the military connotations are evident in the *parleying starlings* (see Notes page 99), and Thomas goes on to set the poem in the context of a broader history. In *'The sun used to shine'* the war intrudes into the idyllic summer Thomas spends with Frost, and then Thomas again broadens the context, setting it against historical conflicts of the past, *the Crusades* and *Caesar's battles* (21–22).

Thomas wrote *'As the team's head brass'* in May of the following year, while at Hare Hall Camp, and this was followed by *Blenheim Oranges* three months later, while he was stationed in London as an officer cadet in the Royal Artillery. Although neither poem is overtly about the war, it is an underlying presence that runs through them both.

Activity

Compare the style and tone of *'As the team's head brass'* and *Blenheim Oranges*, and consider how Thomas presents his ideas in the poems.

Discussion

Neither of these poems is a 'war poem' in the generally accepted sense, but there is an ever-present awareness of the war in both. When *'As the team's head brass'* was written Thomas was still very much working through his feelings about the war and, as Stan Smith (see Further Reading) puts it, the war 'exists beyond the poem's edges' (*Edward Thomas*, page 194). However, the setting of the poem is very far removed from the battlefields of France, and the opening lines are suggestive of the natural cycle of the agricultural world, coupled with an image of human love: *As the team's head brass flashed out on the turn / The lovers disappeared into the wood.*

Both the agricultural round that is part of the cycle of the natural world and the presence of human love suggest permanence and rootedness. The image of the lovers and the wood here is an important one. For Thomas, the wood often represents darkness and death, and here it is clearly contrasted against an image of life. Although the lovers disappear *into the wood*, it is significant that towards the end of the poem they emerge from it again (33), perhaps suggesting that no matter what dark forces threaten it, the life force will continue undiminished.

The war is never far away in this poem and even where the poet sits, *among the boughs of the fallen elm* (3), has been determined by the conflict, as the fallen tree would have been removed were it not for the war. It will not be moved now until the war is over; as in *In Memoriam*, all the young men are gone, fighting in France, and so the natural order of things has been disrupted. As Smith points out:

> The whole poem is full of such disjunctions, whether in the conversation of the two men, or the disruption of work patterns caused by the blizzard, which comes to seem a natural precedent for that larger dislocation effected by the war – a dislocation which has its consequences even at the microcosmic level, since the tree's fall interrupts the customary rhythms and cannot be made good until the war is over.
>
> (*Edward Thomas*, page 194)

Thomas in uniform at Steep, April 1916

The conversation between the poet and the ploughman is initially about the weather, obviously important to rural life, but it quickly turns to the war. Note the suggestion from the ploughman here that the narrator perhaps is avoiding going out to France himself. He becomes absorbed in placing himself in the position of a soldier, and he considers the physical injuries he could sustain – note the repetition of the pronoun *I* in lines 19–22, which intensifies the focus on himself, and the repeated use of *could* and *should*, suggesting that he feels an inner sense of obligation that he should go.

The ploughman's comments on the young men from the area who have gone to France to fight is brought to a personal level when he mentions one of his *mates* who has been killed, *The very night of the blizzard* (27) that had brought down the elm the narrator is now sitting on. He comments that if the war had not happened, and the ploughman's mate had stayed, *Everything / Would have been different. For it would have been / Another world* (29–31).

Note how Thomas has emphasized here the interrelatedness of the war, the natural world and its cycle of life and human love.

The poem ends on, perhaps, a note of uncertainty:

The lovers came out of the wood again:
The horses started and for the last time
I watched the clods crumble and topple over
After the ploughshare and the stumbling team.

(lines 33–36)

Both the lovers emerging from the wood and the ploughman completing his ploughing, which makes the field ready for sowing the next crop, suggest a renewal of life as a new cycle begins. However, this sense of renewal seems tempered with uncertainty. The horses starting *for the last time* has an element of ambiguity and some have suggested that it is the poet who is watching this for the last time, as he knows he will soon be leaving for France with the possibility of never returning. Others, though, see these lines as Thomas recognizing that rural life will never be the same again and that developing mechanization will change the centuries-old ways of life in the English countryside forever. The language used here (*crumble*, *topple over*, *stumbling*) is suggestive of something coming to an end or failing. Thomas's true meaning lies, perhaps, in all these things. As Motion puts it, 'the regeneration within destruction, the hope within apprehension' emerges throughout the poem. 'It provides a complete expression of his ability to suggest alternative interpretations of any given event, and illustrates the range of his war poetry by relating immediate circumstances to recurrent patterns of human and seasonal life' (*The Poetry of Edward Thomas*, page 113).

Blenheim Oranges also evokes a strong sense of change and of time moving on. The repetition of *gone* in the opening line immediately creates the impression of something having passed. In the poem the word refers to the passing of summer, but it is clear that both the line and the poem as a whole have a much broader meaning. Like *'As the team's head brass'*, this poem has suggestions of regeneration. The passing of summer itself is merely a stage in the cycle of nature, and as one season passes into another, new life will eventually come. Nevertheless, there is a sense of emptiness – the months have gone by but they are *Not memorable* (5) except for the fact that he has seen them go, *As past the empty quays / The rivers flow* (7–8), suggesting the narrator is a passive observer. It has been suggested that perhaps this reflects Thomas's feelings about his own role in the war at this stage.

Like the unmoved elm in *'As the team's head brass'*, the apples in the orchard have been left on the tree unpicked, perhaps because labour is in short supply – all the young men who would have picked them are fighting in France. The apples have remained on the tree to be eaten by grubs until the *harvest rain* (10) causes them to fall to the ground. Note how here, as in *'As the team's head brass'*, Thomas presents opposing ideas: the harvest rain would normally be associated with fruitful wholesomeness, but here it causes the *grubby* apples to fall to the ground where they will rot (12). The men who would have harvested the apples have gone to a war that turns *young men to dung* (16). This brutal and graphic metaphor also has connotations of rebirth and regeneration (since dung is used as fertilizer) and creates a sense of new life springing from death. The idea of death is also present in the metaphor of the house, *Dark and untenanted, / With grass growing instead / Of the footsteps of life* (19–21).

The narrator imagines the lives that have been spent in the house, which, like the river flowing, have passed through *Youth, love, age and pain* (24), the cycle of life. He likens himself to the house, almost becomes one with it:

> I am something like that;
> Only I am not dead,
> Still breathing and interested
> In the house that is not dark

(lines 25–28)

The repetition of the line *I am something like that* at the start of the following stanza reinforces his identification with the house, and the final lines of the poem have a sense of bleakness to them: *Not one pane to reflect the sun, / For the schoolboys to throw at – / They have broken every one* (30–32). Some have interpreted these final lines as containing a note of resignation, perhaps reflecting what Thomas was feeling himself at this point. He had chosen to go to France and face his own possible death. As in *'As the team's head brass'*, there is perhaps a sense of possible regeneration here, but if so it is a regeneration achieved through the sacrifice of self: 'He is not dead but the way to the future lies through his death... That Thomas should see his death as part of the conflagration from which the phoenix might rise, explains, perhaps, the tenacity, the integrity of his commitment' (Stan Smith, *Edward Thomas*, page 207).

In the early part of 1916 Thomas was at Hare Hall Camp in Essex where he was a map-reading instructor. Thomas wrote several poems here including '*Home*' and *Thaw*. Longley has described '*Home*' as 'Thomas's most direct poetic reflection on his life as a soldier' (*Edward Thomas: The Annotated Collected Poems*, page 282). In it he conveys a sense of being away from his familiar surroundings and also the feeling of belonging that it gave him, while at the same time recognizing the transitory nature of his comradeship with his fellow soldiers. He had written about his life at the camp and the notion of 'homesickness' to Eleanor Farjeon:

> We are kept much indoors by weather unsuitable for mapping. This is Sunday a wet thawing Sunday but just a day when few know what to do unless they are on leave. Somebody said something about homesickness the other day. It is a disease one can suppress but not do without under these conditions.
> (*Edward Thomas: The Last Four Years*, page 188)

The short poem *Thaw*, consisting of a single quatrain, was written immediately after '*Home*' and has been described as 'an upbeat coda' to the previous poem (see Notes page 101).

Activity

What does *'Home'* tell you about Thomas's feelings, and in what way do you think *Thaw* acts as a concluding part to it?

Discussion

Perhaps the first thing to note about *'Home'* is the title, and the fact that Thomas particularly drew attention to it by placing it in inverted commas. This suggests, as a number of critics have observed, that Thomas is focusing on the word itself and what it means. The poem opens as the narrator and two companions walk in the Surrey countryside. The repetition here of *fair* to describe the weather, their tempers and the countryside around them gives the men a feeling of positivity in a landscape that was strange and that the *untrodden snow* had *made / Wild* and untouched (3–4). The snow has, for the moment at least, made the land *wild and rustic and old* (5), has returned it to the state of old England, and it is as if they are the first to set foot on it. The enjoyment of the men in this environment is emphasized through their singing, an act that also unifies them. This feeling is further reinforced through the repeated use of the plural pronoun *we*.

As they return to the camp, *the cold roofs where we must spend the night* come into view (12). Necessarily their journey has brought them back to their starting point. The walk has given them the impression of freedom, but they are bound to return to the camp just as they are bound by their military duty. The narrator is clearly well aware of this and of the fact that they have not been happy there under the *cold roofs*, but he also recognizes that they had *tasted sleep and food and fellowship / Together long* (14–15). The word 'home', used to describe their destination, the camp, *raised a smile in us all three* (17), and someone repeated the word, smiling again – all three men are clearly aware of the irony of that word applied to the army camp. In one sense, though, the camp is indeed 'home'. Although they are in many respects strangers, the war has brought them together into a kind of *union*:

> Between three countries far apart that lay
> We were divided and looked strangely each
> At the other, and we knew we were not friends

> But fellows in a union that ends
> With the necessity for it, as it ought.

(lines 20–24)

Thomas now switches from *we* to *I* as the narrator ponders on the word 'home' and the common response it has provoked in the men, and on the word 'homesick'. He realizes that:

> If I should ever more admit
> Than the mere word I could not endure it
> For a day longer: this captivity
> Must somehow come to an end, else I should be
> Another man, as often now I seem,
> Or this life be only an evil dream.

(lines 30–35)

To endure his situation and retain his sense of his own identity, he cannot admit to his true feelings until *this captivity* comes to *an end*.

In *Thaw*, the tone becomes more optimistic as the snow is melting and the *speculating rooks at their nests cawed*, as they know that spring is approaching and will bring new life. The rooks see what the human beings below cannot see: *Winter pass*. This idea of birds seeing in the natural world things that go unseen by humans is one that Thomas uses in other poems too, for example *The Glory*, where the *blackbird* and the *dove* (3) find communion with the natural world that Thomas himself seeks.

Among the last poems Thomas wrote were *Lights Out* and *'Out in the dark over the snow'*. *Lights Out* was written in early November 1916, just two months before Thomas went out to France. In several poems he writes about the various bugle calls that governed the day in the camp. For example, in *Cock-Crow* he writes about waking at daybreak, and combines the rural imagery of the cock crowing and the milkers lacing up their boots on the farms with the military *trumpeters* and *coat of arms* (5–7). In *Lights Out*, however, the tone is different and, as in *Rain*, there is an expression of despair. The title of the poem refers to the bugle call signalling to troops in camp to turn out their lights in preparation for sleep. In a letter to Eleanor Farjeon dated 6 November, he told her that the poem 'sums up what I have often thought at that call' (*Edward Thomas: The Last Four Years*, page 218).

'*Out in the dark over the snow*' was written on 24 December and is the last but one poem that Thomas wrote.

Activity

How does Thomas achieve his effects in *Lights Out*?

Discussion

On the surface this is a poem about going to sleep, but sleep here can be seen as a metaphor for death. He describes the sleep as:

> The unfathomable deep
> Forest, where all must lose
> Their way, however straight
> Or winding, soon or late;
> They can not choose.

(lines 2–6)

Often, images of sleep or the forest are used in Thomas's poetry as symbols of death, and here the two combine to create a sense of the inevitability of death – *all* must lose their way in the forest, no matter what paths they have taken in life.

The roads and tracks that the traveller through life takes, the choices made in life, are in a sense illusory – they all lead *to the forest brink* (9) and in that forest *they sink* (12) and all ends:

> Here love ends –
> Despair, ambition ends;

157

> All pleasure and all trouble,
> Although most sweet or bitter,
> Here ends
>
> (lines 13–17)

All things, even *tasks most noble* end in the *sleep that is sweeter* (17–18).

In the penultimate stanza the narrator returns to the things that mean most to him in life, books (literature has been his life) and those whom he loves. He would turn from them now, though, to *go into the unknown*, even though he must do this alone, it will be hard, and he does not know how he is going to achieve it.

In the final stanza, the narrator approaches the edge of the forest, so close its *cloudy foliage lowers / Ahead* (26–27). Note his use of *cloudy* here to suggest a sense of an obscuring element reminiscent of *blurs* in stanza 2. There is a sense of the forest being all-consuming: it *towers* and its *foliage lowers*. He can *hear* its *silence* and he *obeys* it (28). Note the change of tone at the end of the poem; the earlier sense of apprehension is gone, and it is replaced with a sense of acceptance, perhaps even relief. As Motion has said of this poem, '*Lights Out* is not an elegantly phrased Romantic longing for escape, but a realistic assessment of Thomas's chances of survival' (*The Poetry of Edward Thomas*, page 126).

'*Out in the dark over the snow*', Thomas's penultimate poem, was written shortly before he left for France, while he was on his final Christmas leave at High Beech.

Activity

Look at '*Out in the dark over the snow*'. How do the ideas explored here compare with those in *Lights Out*?

Discussion

Like *Lights Out*, '*Out in the dark over the snow*' also presents a contemplation of death. Here the darkness itself seems symbolic of death. However, in this poem Thomas creates a more sinister atmosphere, as the personification of darkness gives it a predatory air, emphasized through the metaphor of a hound hunting him down:

Stealthily the dark haunts round
And, when the lamp goes, without sound
At a swifter bound
Than the swiftest hound,
Arrives, and all else is drowned

(lines 6–10)

The world of light, of life and consciousness is *drowned* by darkness – the darkness is all-consuming, *And I and star and wind and deer / Are in the dark together* (lines 11–12).

There is a sense of fear of the darkness here too, leading to the final, bleak stanza in which the narrator sees how weak light is in the conscious universe, how all things, even *Love and delight* (18), are consumed by the darkness. The very sound of the poem, with its single rhythm in each stanza, blankets the poem in a repetitive, monotonous 'sameness' which, like the darkness itself, draws all light and life from the poem.

Thomas had made his choices by now and taken his own path, but he felt that whichever road was taken the end result would be the same. In his poem *Roads* he explores the nature of roads, a favourite symbol of his. In the poem, he knows that for him:

Now all roads lead to France
And heavy is the tread
Of the living; but the dead
Returning lightly dance

(lines 53–56)

Edward Thomas in 1914

Critical views

When the first collection of Thomas's poems appeared in October 1917, they received a positive reception from several quarters, including a review in *The Times Literary Supplement*. His friends, particularly Walter de la Mare and Robert Frost, also spoke positively of his work, and over the next few years there were a number of favourable reviews from the critics. Few of these, however, fully recognized in Thomas's poetry his true achievements, and there was limited recognition of the contribution his work made to the evolution of modern poetry. Critics preferred to see him as having more in common with the now outmoded Georgian poets (see page 107), who had fallen from favour even in Thomas's lifetime, than the modernism of Pound or Eliot. Other positive reviews followed, but again very few of them saw Thomas's work in the context of the more modern trends in poetry and criticism.

In 1920, J. Middleton Murry, the literary critic and editor of *Rhyme* magazine, wrote a piece praising Thomas's search for the truth in his poetry (see Further Reading), comparing him favourably with Keats, and commenting that had he lived to perfect his poetry, 'he might have been a great poet indeed'. He did not live to perfect it, however, and so Middleton Murry concludes that he is 'not a great poet... but one who had many of the qualities of a great poet' ('The Poetry of Edward Thomas', 1920).

That remained the general view for many until another perspective was offered by the influential (and at times controversial) academic and critic, F.R. Leavis. In 1932 he published his *New Bearings in English Poetry*, a survey of the literature of the first part of the twentieth century. Leavis recognized Thomas as an important figure in modern poetry and pointed to the error made by those who insisted on regarding him as a Georgian poet, as well as indicating the qualities that make him unquestionably a modern poet: 'only a very superficial classification could associate Edward Thomas... with the Georgians at all. He was a very original poet who devoted great technical subtlety to the expression of a distinctly modern sensibility' (*New Bearings in English Poetry*, page 55).

Welcome though this recognition was it did little to increase interest in Thomas's poetry, and some later critics still insisted on seeing him as, basically, a Georgian poet. However, in 1954 Cecil Day-Lewis, later to become Poet Laureate, delivered a lecture (later published as an essay) in which he assessed the poetry of Thomas. He recalls, how, in his last year at Oxford, he and W.H. Auden drew up a list of 'contemporary poets whom we had little or no hope of ever equalling'. It was a very short list, but one of the names on it was that of Edward Thomas. Despite this kind of praise, many still regarded Thomas as a minor poet, partly because of the limited number of poems he had produced and partly because some saw his poetry as being too personal in nature to achieve the broader and deeper significance of 'great' poetry.

In 1985, R.G. Thomas published his *Edward Thomas: A Portrait*, the first in-depth biography of Thomas, and since then a growing number of both critical and biographical works on the life and work of the poet have appeared. These have increased interest in Thomas and helped to develop an understanding of the complexities of both the man and his work. The work of Edna Longley has done much to further this knowledge in recent years, through her *Edward Thomas: Poems and Last Poems* (1973) and *The Annotated Collected Poems* (2008).

In 1980, Andrew Motion's *The Poetry of Edward Thomas* appeared, at the time the only study entirely on the work of Thomas as a poet. This has now been joined by others, such as Michael Kirkham's *The Imagination of Edward Thomas* (1986) and Judy Kendall's *Edward Thomas: The Origins of His Poetry* (2012). Matthew Hollis's biography *Now All Roads Lead to France: The Last Years of Edward Thomas* (2011), covering the last four years of Thomas's life, has been widely acclaimed, and its serialization as BBC Radio 4's Book of the Week no doubt contributed to bringing an awareness of the life and work of Edward Thomas to a new audience.

Essay Questions

1 *We look and understand,*
   We cannot speak
   Except in trifles and
   Words the most weak.

   Discuss the ways in which Thomas presents his feelings in
   'No one so much as you'. In your answer, explore the effects
   of language, imagery and verse form, and consider how
   this poem relates to other poems by Thomas you have
   studied.

2 Discuss the ways in which Thomas explores ideas about
   memory in his poetry. In your answer, you should write
   about **two** or **three** poems you have studied.

3 *Now I know that Spring will come again,*
   Perhaps tomorrow.

   Discuss the ways in which spring is important in Thomas's
   poetry. In your answer, you should write about *March* and
   one or **two** other poems you have studied.

4 Explore Thomas's use of symbolism in *The Hollow Wood* and
   in **one** or **two** other poems you have studied.

5 *When these old woods were young*
   The thrushes' ancestors
   As sweetly sung
   In the old years.

   Discuss the ways in which birdsong is important in *Under
   the Wood*. In your answer, explore the effects of language,
   imagery and verse form, and consider how this poem relates
   to other poems by Thomas you have studied.

6 *What I desired I knew not, but whate'er my choice*
 Vain it must be.

 Discuss the ways in which Thomas presents his feelings and state of mind in *Melancholy*. In your answer, explore the effects of language, imagery and verse form, and consider how this poem relates to other poems by Thomas you have studied.

7 *I know you:*
 You are light as dreams,
 Tough as oak.

 Discuss how Thomas presents his ideas about language in *Words* and **one** or **two** other poems by you have studied.

8 Explore how Thomas presents his thoughts and feelings about England in his poetry. In your answer, you should write about **two** or **three** poems you have studied.

9 *That fine day, May the twenty-third,*
 The day Jack Noman disappeared.

 Discuss the importance of the 'solitary figure' in *May 23* and **one** other poem by Thomas you have studied.

10 Explore the ways in which Thomas's sense of 'patriotism' is presented in **two** or **three** poems you have studied.

11 *Whatever wind blows, while they and I have leaves*
 We cannot other than an aspen be.

 Discuss the ways in which Thomas uses the aspen trees to explore ideas about his own state of mind in *Aspens*. In your answer, explore the effects of language, imagery and verse form, and consider how this poem relates to other poems by Thomas you have studied.

12 Discuss how Thomas presents his attitude towards the war in *'This is no case of petty right or wrong'* and **one** or **two** other poems you have studied.

13 *We turned from men or poetry*
To rumours of the war remote.

Explore the ways in which Thomas presents his ideas in
'*The sun used to shine*'. In your answer, explore the effects
of language, imagery and verse form, and consider how this
poem relates to other poems by Thomas you have studied.

14 *Here love ends –*
Despair, ambition ends.

Explore the ways in which Thomas presents ideas about
death in *Lights Out* and **one** or **two** other poems you have
studied.

15 Explore the ways in which Thomas's presentation of the
natural world is important in his poetry. In your answer you
should write about **two** or **three** poems you have studied.

Chronology

1878   Philip Edward Thomas born on 3 March in Lambeth, London, the eldest son of Philip Henry and Mary Elizabeth Thomas. Both parents had been brought up in Wales.

1883–93   Educated at various schools including Battersea Grammar School. During this time the family spent holidays in Wales and Wiltshire.

1894   Thomas's father moves him to St Paul's School, Hammersmith with the intention of educating him for the civil service. Thomas is resistant to this idea. While at St Paul's he visits the writer and critic James Ashcroft Noble, who encourages him in his writing.

1895   Leaves St Paul's School. Some of his essays are published in various publications, and he develops a friendship with Noble's daughter, Helen.

1896   Helen's father dies. Thomas works towards entry to Oxford University.

1897   His first book, *The Woodland Life*, is published.

1898   Wins a scholarship to Lincoln College, Oxford.

1899   He and Helen are married in June at Fulham Registry Office.

1900   Their son Merfyn born in January. In the summer Thomas gains a second-class degree in history.

1901   Moves from Balham to Rose Acre Cottage near Bearsted in Kent.

1902   Publishes a collection of essays, *Horae Solitariae*. Daughter Bronwen born in October.

1903   Receives a first commission for a book, *Oxford*. The family move a short distance to Ivy Cottage, Bearsted.

1904   The family move again, to Elses Farm, near Sevenoaks in Kent. Receives another commission, this time to write *Beautiful Wales*.

1905   *Beautiful Wales* published and he continues a punishing schedule of writing commissioned books and reviewing, which lead to him suffering from mental and physical exhaustion.

1906   *The Heart of England* published. Meets W.H. Hudson and Walter de la Mare. The family move to Berryfield Cottage, near Petersfield in Hampshire.

1907   Consults a doctor about his depression: 'melancholia', as he calls it.

1908   Suffers more depression and ill-health.

1909   *Richard Jefferies* and *The South Country* published. Moves to Wick Green, near Petersfield.

1910   *Feminine Influence on the Poets, Windsor Castle,* and *Rest and Unrest* published. In August, their second daughter Myfanwy born.

1911   *The Isle of Wight, Light and Twilight, Maurice Maeterlinck, Celtic Stories,* and *The Tenth Muse* published. Thomas suffers a mental breakdown caused by overwork and financial worries.

1912   *Algernon Charles Swinburne, George Borrow: The Man and His Books, Lafcadio Hearn* and *Norse Tales* published. Receives treatment for depression. Meets Eleanor Farjeon.

1913   The family move to Yew Tree Cottage in Steep. *The Country, The Icknield Way. The Happy-Go-Lucky Morgans* and *Walter Pater* published. In October Thomas meets Robert Frost.

1914   *In Pursuit of Spring* published and Thomas reviews Frost's second published collection of poetry, *North of Boston.* The Thomas and Frost families spend August together at Leddington, near Ledbury. 4 August: Britain declares war on Germany. Thomas considers going to America with Frost. In December Thomas starts to write poetry.

1915　In February, when Frost returns to America, Merfyn returns with him to visit a former headmaster who now lives there. In July Thomas enlists and joins the Artists' Rifles, and in November is a map-reading instructor at Hare Hall, Essex. *Four-and-Twenty Blackbirds*, *The Life of the Duke of Marlborough*, and *This England* published.

1916　*Keats* published. Thomas becomes an officer cadet at the Royal Artillery School, London. The Thomas family move to High Beech, Essex. In November Thomas is commissioned as a second lieutenant and posted to 244 Siege Battery, Kent. He volunteers for service overseas.

1917　January: 'Last poem' written in his diary. Leaves for France. In March *An Annual of New Poetry* is published containing some of his poems under the pseudonym Edward Eastaway. April: involved in preparations for battle. On Easter Monday, 9 April, the first day of the Battle of Arras, soon after 7.30 am, Thomas is killed by a shell blast while directing the fire of his battery. October: his volume, *Poems*, published.

1918　*Last Poems* published.

1920　*Collected Poems* published.

Further Reading

Poetry editions

William Cooke (ed.), *Edward Thomas* (Everyman, 1997)

Matthew Hollis (ed.), *Edward Thomas: Selected Poems* (Faber & Faber, 2011)

Judy Kendall (ed.), *Edward Thomas's Poets* (Carcanet, 2007)

Edna Longley (ed.), *Edward Thomas: Poems and Last Poems* (Macdonald and Evans, 1973)

Edna Longley (ed.), *Edward Thomas: The Annotated Collected Poems* (Bloodaxe, 2008)

R. George Thomas (ed.), *Edward Thomas: Collected Poems* (Faber & Faber, 2004)

R.S. Thomas (ed.), *Selected Poems of Edward Thomas* (Faber & Faber, 1964)

A selection of Thomas's prose writing

The South Country (Little Toller Books, 2009; first published J.M. Dent, 1909)

Feminine Influence on the Poets (John Lane, 1911, available through Google Books; first published Martin Secker, 1910)

The Icknield Way (Constable, 1913, available through Google Books)

In Pursuit of Spring (Laurel Books, 2002; first published Thomas Nelson & Sons, 1914)

Biography

Eleanor Farjeon, *Edward Thomas: The Last Four Years* (OUP, 1958; Faber & Faber, 2010)

Matthew Hollis, *Now All Roads Lead to France: The Last Years of Edward Thomas* (Faber & Faber, 2011)

Helen Thomas and Myfanwy Thomas, *Under Storm's Wing* (Carcanet, 1988)

R. George Thomas, *Edward Thomas: A Portrait* (Oxford University Press, 1985)

Criticism

Theresa Ashton, 'Edward Thomas: From Prose to Poetry', in *The Poetry Review* 28, November–December 1937

Cecil Day-Lewis, 'The Poetry of Edward Thomas', in *Essays by Divers Hands*, ed. Angela Thirkell (Oxford University Press, 1956)

Judy Kendall, *Edward Thomas: The Origins of His Poetry* (University of Wales Press, 2012)

Michael Kirkham, *The Imagination of Edward Thomas* (Cambridge University Press, 1986)

F.R. Leavis, *New Bearings in English Poetry* (Pelican Books 1972; first published Chatto & Windus, 1932)

J. Middleton Murry, 'The Poetry of Edward Thomas', in *Aspects of Literature* (Collins, 1920)

Andrew Motion, *The Poetry of Edward Thomas* (Routledge & Kegan Paul, 1980)

Stan Smith, *Edward Thomas* (Faber & Faber, 1986)

Websites

Edward Thomas Fellowship: www.edward-thomas-fellowship.org.uk

First World War Poetry Digital Archive: www.oucs.ox.ac.uk/ww1lit/collections

Friends of the Dymock Poets: www.dymockpoets.co.uk